Guided Migrations

A Search for Healing through
the Journey of Life

Kristin Wall Buchholz

Hyssop Press

This story would not have been written without the love of my life, Dan Allen, whose caring and support allows me the time and inspiration needed to create. I am truly thankful for my daughter Ada, who saves my life again and again, bringing me hope and the need to be a better person, and for my step-son Riley who I love dearly. I am grateful for the parents I was given, for their love and best efforts, even if I needed more. I wish to express deep gratitude to the people who loved and befriended me along the way: Jody Masciangelo and her entire family, Alysia Kovitch, Raymond Loh, Cindi Kelly, Cassandra Robbers, Sandy and Don Cameron, Judy and Bob Loughlin, Velma Smith Buchholz, and Michele Friedman. I have deep gratitude for all my teachers from the Arts, through university, and into the vast world of Yoga. Michele, no one would read these words without your brilliant editing, loving guidance, and fierce support. For all of you, for my angels and ancestors, I am forever grateful.

Table of Contents

Preface

For the past two decades or so, I've been lucky enough to learn yoga and meditation from many wonderful teachers. I wish to thank Krishna Das, Ram Das, Lana Reed and Kartar Khalsa, Lisa Broderick, Dharma Mittra, MC Yogi, Ajeet, Catherine Cook Cottone, Staci Curry, Gena Decker, Raymond Loh, and Cindi Kelly, to name a few. Most of the names in this story have been changed to respect privacy and acknowledge that they have their own stories and perspectives to share. Whether sweet or sour, they've all given me valuable lessons for which I am perpetually grateful.

Today, I benefit from an hour of yoga and meditation each morning, which took many years to develop. What started it all for me was three minutes on the mat. For a long time, I was resentful with life. I was angry that I gave so much of my life away every day. I felt panicked every Sunday night when my weekend of freedom drew to a close and I hadn't reached the bottom of my to-do list where my needs were written.

Instead, I started to place yoga at the top of every list I made and promised to give myself at least three minutes of my day, every day. From those three minutes, this story grew. This story is dedicated to anyone who feels lost, invisible, or without hope. It doesn't take as long as three minutes, really, it can be discovered in a single breath, if you're present. For most of us, though, it may take a lifetime to turn inward. I encourage you to start today. Everything you seek is there.

Om Peace. Namaste. Shanti. Shanti. Shanti.

Introduction

When I was a kid, I witnessed the lives of adults around me as one might observe fascinating animals in captivity: with wonder, curiosity, and some measure of unspeakable love and empathy. I watched adults at home, at church, in school, at grocery stores, restaurants, on city streets, at summer camps, sporting events, in movies, and on television. Often, I would think, "Just look at how sad they are, fumbling around, not knowing how to get out of the trap they're in." There seemed to be a connection with what adults did for a living, (what their job title or role in society was) with their level of satisfaction or happiness in life. Or maybe, this connection was pure fantasy adults had invented and continued to delude themselves with. In any case, two answers began to emerge and form simultaneously, one spoken and one silent, to the ubiquitous question "What do you want to be when you grow up?"

My verbal answer might have changed from "Teacher, ice-skater, or artist," but the silent answer was always the same. I wanted to be happy. Happy adults seemed to be rare and linked, not just with their job, but with an individual's sense of freedom as well as the health of their relationships. If you're happy, you've found equanimity in life, so why worry about which job you choose? If you focus on being happy and healthy, all the complicated stuff like employment will sort itself out as you go, or at least I hoped it would.

The first time I remember feeling truly happy, I was about four years old. I experienced an innate sense of oneness with nature. Exploring the natural world was captivating and joyful. Sunlight on tall grasses moving in a breeze, the conversations in birdsong, fish leading mysterious lives in the murky depths of our small pond, all swept me up with genuine wonder, awe and spontaneous feelings of joy. I felt seen and heard by the infinite forms of life surrounding me. I was doing my thing, being a curious human, full of awe and delight, and everything else was too. We each had a role to play and jobs to do. I joined in with bird calls and felt heard, and more importantly, accepted as part of the glorious eco-tapestry I was exploring. I crept slowly down the path toward the pond, admiring the diversity of wildflowers and native plants, all uniquely rooted in their place, participating in this collective harmony. Listening to the insects near and far, the landscape of sounds deepened as I approached the pond. The calls of spring peepers and bullfrogs welcomed me.

Statuesque and almost threatening, stood the Great Blue Heron on the opposite side of our pond. It took a while for me to notice its presence, to acknowledge that we were sharing this lovely little pond. Gradually, I became aware that the Heron had been watching me for some time. We witnessed one another. In that moment, we were one, and I was truly, undeniably happy. The word happy seems trite, selfish even. This was bigger, more connected; an integrated, whole-body bliss. I was seen by the Heron; somehow acknowledged as part of the beauty all around me. I can still recall images from these early years and how I felt, before everything changed. Decades later the Heron would return and remind me of my place in the world of the living.

After my parents divorced, my mom, brother, and I moved nearly every year, just trying to make it, I guess. We were like modern-day vagabonds, schlepping our stuff from one apartment to the next, never staying long enough to get to know the neighbors or put down any roots. A popular joke back then was, "Hey, I saw yo' mama kickin' a can down the street. I said, 'Whatcha doin'? And she said, 'Movin'." I never liked it much, because I thought it was about *us*. My mom had stuff, at least. She had a large Norfolk Pine in a pot, and some sharp Mother-in-law's Tongues that we brought along each time we moved. I guess there was some comfort in having the same plants and pictures, the same knick-knacks and Christmas decorations as a way to create some cohesion from place to place. Perhaps it was my mom's way of bringing mother nature with us wherever we went. As I grew, though, I couldn't shake the feeling of utter contrast. The bright, blissful freedom of my past, experiencing oneness with nature, being seen by the Great Blue Heron, and feeling securely rooted to a place that was much greater than myself; to the darkness of not knowing where home was or where we'd go next, or why, like a potted plant held captive and kept alive but never rooted, never truly thriving.

I found safety in making my own forts inside of closets. Most every apartment we moved into had some sort of narrow closet with an accordion door that I could hide in. I'd spread out a sleeping bag on the floor, hang a Michael Jackson or Madonna poster on the wall beneath the hanging clothes and plug in a clip-lamp so I could read or draw there in peace. I remember feeling safer in these smaller spaces where, if someone stepped into the room, they wouldn't know I was there. These spaces were my own sanctuaries that made me feel safe and protected, not only from our ever-changing living situation, but from the stress-responses we all experienced.

There was often yelling, slamming doors, arguments between my brother and me, which felt stressful. My mother, exhausted after long days in the office, lacked the parenting skills or support she needed to raise us with the love and emotional connection we deserved, left us all with unmet needs. This unstable and sometimes volatile homelife left me insecure, longing for loving connection. Also, I was smaller than my peers. One long-time baby-sitter who watched me after school through my elementary years called me "Peanut," because I was more petite than other kids. I grew into my own, healthy stature in time, but long after most other kids in my grade. Being different in this way added to my insecurity, and I longed for my father's reassurance and guidance growing up.

Even though he was alive and well and we saw him on the weekends, our father chose not to be a part of our lives unless it was mandated by the court. This fact was a heavy darkness that settled over my life for many years. Compounding this sorrow was the confusion of not knowing why my parents divorced. Years later, my mom remarried. I was vaguely aware that my stepfather, Ernest, used to be our neighbor, but I didn't know the whole story. One of my new step sisters, Stephanie, took me for a long walk one day, which was very unusual. Normally she wanted nothing to do with me. I remember our sun-dappled walking path through tall trees that everyone called the "trolley bed." On this meandering walk, Stephanie told me that my mom had an affair with her dad, and that's why we were living together. It came as a shock to me then, at about eight years old, but I'd known for a long time that my mom kept things from me because I was too young, or because I was a girl, or both. Stephanie was about sixteen then, and had no reason to lie, but I sensed that she enjoyed bursting my bubble at that moment. She hated my mom and the feeling was mutual. Telling me the truth about our family may have been motivated by some need for revenge against these adults she despised. Stephanie was a rebel, always in trouble, often arguing with her dad. One time the police brought her home. I remember hearing arguments about me sharing a room with her and her older sister, Victoria, after that. I'm sure they didn't want me there either. It felt as though my father had rejected me, and so did my new step sisters. Not only did I feel disconnected from nature in the suburbs, I was also disconnected from myself. I began to believe that I was an unwanted burden and terribly flawed, so much so that I cried myself to sleep every night longing for that blissful, childhood home, and life with my dad. This destructive cry-sleep ritual lasted for many years. My sleep was so disturbed that once I woke up attempting to climb into a dresser drawer. Sleepwalking was uncommon for me, but restless, disturbed sleep was my norm. My mom did her best to keep this new family balanced and happy, but there was too much animosity, and too little communication.

This new marriage and new family unit did not last, and we moved again after a couple of years. My mom may have had an affair with my stepfather, but that didn't mean she wanted to be with him for the rest of her life. When my father wouldn't forgive her or even try to work things out, she decided to remarry thinking it was the right thing to do. He was a wonderful man, my stepfather, but my mom didn't love him like she loved our father. It was over before it even started. The nice house in the suburban neighborhood with a backyard and other kids to play with was gone in the blink of an eye, and so were our older stepsisters. We never saw them again.

For decades, my life had two distinct sides: this life with my mom and what she was doing, where she was living, who she was with in the suburbs, and the other side consisting of my father, his family, and his childhood home in the Southern Tier. My brother and I lived with our mom and stayed mostly on this side of life, with her rules and expectations. On weekends, we'd fit ourselves into the sliver of life that had our father in it, with different rules, and different expectations. For example, at my mom's there was a hard rule that you took your shoes off right after you walked through the door. No outdoor shoes could go a step further. At dad's house, you kept your shoes on. Often, we were told this after we had already taken off our shoes, so we had to put them back on while listening to why keeping your shoes on in their house was so important. There were a few other contradictory rules, but mostly I remember being shoved into the middle in conversations about the other parent, and I hated that. It tore me up inside having to listen to my stepmother trash talk my mom and not be able to defend her or speak up about how I felt. If it weren't for close friends like Jody (whose loving, Italian family practically adopted me from the fourth grade through graduation) and my cousin, Alysia, I don't know if or where I would be today.

Life clipped on through grade school with the usual stuff. Dinner, homework, talking on the phone to friends, shower, and bed. In the '70s and '80s, social media was the telephone anchored to the wall. We had slow, rotary dial phones and later on, the modern push-button version, usually in a black or beige finish, but all secured to a wall. When you talked on the phone you were tethered to one place and could not always multitask like we do today. Often, I would lay back on my bed and slide my legs up the wall while I talked on the phone, or listened, mostly, since I wasn't much of a talker back then. I remember telling Jody about a recent visit to the Southern Tier, which my friends in the suburbs knew nothing about.

My father, his three sisters, and older brother grew up in the town of Whitesville in Allegany County, just minutes from the Pennsylvania border in the foothills of Appalachia. A small, rural town doesn't come close to describing Whitesville. When my dad was in high school there, the town was enjoying its peak with thirty-five or more students graduating in each class. Today it's more like eight to ten students in each graduating class and they've had to downsize to Kindergarten through eighth grades, because they can't find enough teachers who will stay and teach on the high school level.

When you drive through town it's like moving through a slow time warp as you pass the old homes, volunteer fire department, tiny brick library, and the one and only general store. The post office still has iron bars on the clerk's desk from over a hundred years ago.

I'm not an expert on the history of Whitesville, although my grandmother was. Velma Smith Buchholz worked her way through nursing school and became the only medical professional in the area for miles around. I loved looking at her black and white graduation photo from nursing school in the 1940s with all the women dressed in wool capes and odd little, origami hats. Velma made house calls like a real doctor and was known and loved by just about everyone in the area. And man, did she have stories. Once, she used cobwebs to stop the bleeding on an injured migrant worker who'd been hurt in a knife fight. Most of her treatments were more practical, however. When her kids had cold and flu symptoms, a spoonful of whiskey and some honey did wonders. "G'won, now," she'd say, "off to bed."

My gram lived and loved large. She had five kids and put herself through college before she reached her late-twenties. Her door was always open and she loved when anyone sat at her round kitchen table to listen to her gab about who was related to whom, where they came from, and what they were up to now. She'd set out a plate of cookies and make tea, open an overstuffed shoebox of family photos and claim the next couple of hours to connect everyone at the table with stories at the center.

Eventually, she became the school nurse for Whitesville Central School and later the town historian. I remember watching her ride on a decorated float in the Memorial Day Parade as senior citizen of the year. She was a smart cookie who loved to talk and had a sharp mind for names and dates. She told me that she thought my father was being a "stubborn German" when he refused to work things out after my mom had an affair with the neighbor. She and my mom were close because everyone was close to my gram. She had infinite space in her heart and her tiny home for anyone who wanted a part of it. Thankfully, because of this, my mom and I continued to visit her in Whitesville as I grew up, and Whitesville, as it slowed and decayed, became an even more special place to me.

Visiting my gram from the stressful suburbs had an instant healing effect on me. Behind her home, is a steep hillside that rises out of old pastures and potato fields my grandfather once farmed. My favorite things to do were to visit the crick and hike up the hill, picking wildflowers along the way. Smelling the sweet, fresh air soothed my mind and calmed my body. With every step, I am reminded of the Heron's gaze, reminded that I too am part of this beautiful world, even if others didn't see it. The steepest sections of the climb came with the strongest reminders, the loudest heartbeats, and resounding breaths. Before making it to the top, my worries and anxieties would dissolve. Tension and worry seemed to melt from my shoulders and seep into the earth, as naturally as rainwater washing down the ditches.

Decades ago, my grandfather sold ten acres to the neighbor, Mr. Flamini. The Flamini boys, always nearby, became close friends with our family, and helped build my Aunt Sandy a cabin for a bit of cash and a lot of beer. About the time of my high school graduation she had a long pond dug and filled it with koi fish, symbols of our ancestors and inspiration for artistic spirits like ours. The Flamini's still look after and care for our land there in Whitesville, mowing, logging when needed, rebuilding washed out bridges, and checking on the fish in the warmer months.

Sandy is one of my dad's three older sisters. She followed in her mother's footsteps and became a nurse, but like her mom, she didn't stop there. She became Town Justice of the Peace for the village of Alfred, as well as a ceramic artist. She had a vision of her own place in nature as she climbed this same hill growing up. She'd found the best spot with an amazing view of the valley looking south into Pennsylvania where her cozy cabin still stands today.

While we waited for rain to fill the newly excavated pond, Sandy and I indulged in a mud bath and laid in the sun until the baked mud cracked on our summer skin. Feeding the fish and walking through the woods did wonders for my soul and do today as well. It was these people, Velma and Sandy, and undoubtedly the forestland on this hill, that grounded me enough to make it through the fear and trauma my childhood offered. Hiking up the hill behind my gram's little house on Main Street made me feel like this was my true home. It's still a place that welcomes me like a daughter, where I feel connected to every living thing, including myself.

Life Before

"How lucky am I to have something that makes saying goodbye so hard." — Winnie the Pooh

"We don't know about tomorrow," said the horse, "all we need to know is that we love each other."
— Charlie Mackesy

A lysia used to cry for days when we had to say goodbye to each other. I didn't realize how truly traumatizing our goodbyes were for her until my fortieth birthday party. She fought to smile through tears as family snapped pictures, and she left me with a wet shoulder after our parting hug. I can see her pain in the photos of us when I look back on that summer day. Since then, she's steadily improved her leave-taking skills, yet she's keenly aware of how this pain is connected to her being abandoned as an infant. She was three months old when my aunt and uncle adopted her. She tells a story about how aware she was of her adoption growing up, as her father joked that he still had the receipt and that he could take her back. Insensitive and harsh, she took this to heart. To her, the message was loud and clear: she'd been abandoned once and could be again at any moment. I was ready to keep her, however. Although we were cousins, what Alysia and I had felt more like sisterhood. We didn't know then that I was the

German girl and she was the Jew. It wouldn't have mattered if we did. We just loved each other immensely. And so do her parents, although she may still be realizing this today.

My husband, Chad, and his mom Roxy (Nana), threw me a big surprise party at her house for my fortieth trip around the sun. I felt honored and very loved. Both our families came and they all made wishes for us and tied them to helium balloons and set them free to fly into the endless blue above. Deep down, I knew this grand gesture was to celebrate our wedding anniversary, which happened to be on the same day as my birthday, but I tried to ignore that fact, as well as how unhappy I was with our marriage. My darling daughter, Ada, was just three and loved every bit of it. How could I disappoint her? Alysia came out from Ohio to be there and loved it just as much.

One of the earliest memories I have of Alysia is playing with her when we were little in her giant, old farmhouse in Alfred, New York. There were huge pocket doors that slid in and out of walls like magic, special hiding places, and her own bedroom filled with fun. We would act out TV shows and soap operas I barely knew anything about and pretended to be sophisticated adults. We played with Barbie dolls, skinny dipped in her backyard pool, and fed her horse Cricket. It was a magical time for me as a kid, or, at least, most highlights of my childhood were spent with my co-star and sister-cousin Alysia. She is still one of the most fabulous, extraordinary people I know.

As kids, we wrote letters to each other almost weekly. When my Uncle Bob got a big promotion at KeyBank, her whole family moved to East Aurora, NY, which seemed wrong to me. I wanted them to stay in the farmhouse on the way to my Gram's in Whitesville. We saw each other a bit less after their move, so being relentless pen pals helped keep us connected. Every summer my father and stepmother took us on a camping trip and we each got to have a cousin-sister or brother along for the adventure. Of course, Alysia and I were thick as thieves and my brother, Freddy, hung out with our cousin Owen, who was kind and easy-going. It took some patience to be with Owen, and Freddy seemed to adjust to his tempo and enjoy his company. Alysia and I zoomed ahead and took every opportunity to go our own way, blaze our own trail, to be left alone at the beach or the lake or the tent, so we could just be on our own together.

When I was seven or eight years old, our cousin Kristy died from Leukemia. Alysia was eight at the time, and Kristy was nine. She was the sweetest, most innocent, beautiful nine-year-old girl you can imagine, with big brown eyes and luxurious brown hair. When it fell out after chemotherapy, my Aunt Jo-Ann tied bandannas around her head and gave her cute hats to wear. We heard whispered horror stories about how painful her treatment was and how it wasn't working. I was not allowed to attend the funeral, which in hindsight, was a good decision. I did not yet comprehend that Kristy was gone forever, but I may have started believing that when I turned nine, I might get cancer and die too, just because it terrified me and survivor's guilt is real.

Through our letters, I felt I could talk to Alysia about it and we soon became best friends, or sister-cousins as we often say. At ten, we played with barbies and other toys. At eleven, we stayed up late playing cards and talking. At twelve, we tried to sneak out of the tent with flashlights, or sneak downstairs for a midnight snack. At thirteen, we gossiped about all the kids at school, who we had crushes on, and who we might want to be with someday. At fourteen, we smoked whatever we could find as we acted out soap operas in our aunt and uncle's lake house. That summer we got dropped off at Sylvan beach together so we could relax in the sun, talk nonstop, and tell grown men to leave us alone, because we were only fourteen! At fifteen or sixteen, we tipped peach schnapps into our orange juice during family gatherings and found the room farthest from the rest of the family so we could be on our own together.

From a distance, it may have looked like Alysia was a bad influence on me, but up close, she was saving me. She saw me, and much like the Heron, always led the way. After our

teen years set in, the camping trips and visits to lakes stopped, so we convinced our mothers that we had to spend a solid week together every summer no matter what. And we did.

We manifested our own, private vacations together every year. We did whatever we wanted, talked and laughed, skinny-dipped and hiked, posed for pictures, reminisced and stayed up as late as we possibly could. One summer at her suburban house in East Aurora, we vowed to stay up all night. We wanted to reminisce about the times we spent at the lake, the little cottage we stayed in together, and every detail about our lives we could think to share with each other. We made a pot of coffee (and yuck, I didn't like coffee yet, but it was supposed to make us feel wide awake, so we went for it and drank a whole pot while we kvetched.) We only made it until four a.m., which was close enough for us.

After that we crashed hard and soon after created a new salutation for our letters; C-C-4 would remind us of our precious times spent at the cottage on the lake, all that coffee we drank, and how we stayed up until four in the morning. A lot like LYLAS, (love ya like a sister, which we already employed) C-C-4 was our very own code that kept us connected, remembering where we'd been together. It seemed like an unbreakable bond, until the unthinkable happened.

I was living in Boston after graduating from art school and Alysia finished her degree at Fredonia before moving to North Carolina. We lost touch. We were busy, indestructible fools in our twenties, raging through life, unstoppable. I worked four different jobs and rode my bike and public transit all over Boston while Alysia partied like a rock star and worked at a salon in Wilmington, North Carolina. We spoke on occasion but had stopped writing to one another years ago. We stopped seeing each other like we had when we were kids, and although we were still connected, we had become strangers.

I remember one phone call we had after too many years of distance. Alysia didn't know if it was 4am or 4pm when I called her. She sounded high, or hungover. I remember feeling stunned, like I didn't know her anymore. I was scared and confused and wanted to be back on her couch sipping coffee and talking. There was this big, ugly chasm between us and I didn't know how to shrink it. Eventually, Alysia leveled out, met a fantastic man (Kevman) and got married. After her wedding, we reconnected. It was like we picked up right where we left off and started spending time together again every summer.

I think it was her idea to spend a long weekend in our Aunt Sandy's cabin in the wilderness of Whitesville, New York. As soon as school let out in June (I'd been teaching art for a few years by then) we'd meet up with way too much stuff and head for the hill. The 120 acres of wilderness behind our grandmother's old house beckoned us every summer. Before this, I always parked in the pasture and hiked up the hill wearing a backpack. When Alysia arrived, she had one bag entirely filled with shoes, one bag of swim gear, a cooler filled with wine and several other bags of clothing and other essentials. I too wanted to be prepared and brought more than I needed. I quickly realized why all the adults in our family drove up the hill to reach the cabin.

At first it was just us, like when we were kids, then we let it grow. Michele was our first invite, and even though she's our cousin's daughter, we saw her as our sister and it was only natural to pull her into the fold. More friends and family began to join us and now, we've got our own lovely tribe deep inside the bigger family. We float in the pond and sneak around trying to catch frogs, sit around bonfires, send up paper lanterns or light up fireworks, walk in the woods and marvel at the sunsets. We soak it all up, the beauty of this life we're in together, drink too much, smoke too much cannabis, and laugh too loud.

These beautiful women talked sense into me when I expressed how unhappy I was in my marriage. I snapped out of the trance I was in because of them. One summer evening under the stars, after we danced around with sparklers, feeling like magic forest fairies, Michele pleaded with me, "If you're not happy with your life, you've gotta *change* it. It's just too important to ignore. And I love you too much to see you unhappy." Because of our trust and our closeness, these words were like fertilizer. I did nothing but let it all grow wild.

Summer on the hill in Whitesville, 2019

Masked Deliveries

"It is the history of our kindnesses that alone make this world tolerable." — Robert Louis Stevenson

Coasting through ghost towns in a gentle, soaking rain, it was the second day I had traveled to nearby towns making deliveries. A few cars, sure, but practically no one was out anywhere. Covid-19 was keeping everyone indoors, especially on bad weather days. Granted, four inches of snow had fallen just a few days ago, and only now was it starting to feel like it should in the Western New York wilds: cold and damp, April showers and all. The snowdrops bloomed and left weeks ago, but the daffodils are still blooming, their heavy heads hanging low; forsythia everywhere displaying its spray of shocking yellow along roadsides. I had a silent fear that their efforts would go unappreciated.

As I drove that day, my thoughts turned to the roadsides of Texas and Southern Utah. Many years ago, I needed to get away. Living in Boston was a wonderful adventure, but I found myself stuck in another codependent relationship. My sense of adventure and need to explore came from my mother, as did my codependency. She loved to travel, to visit new places, and experience all it had to offer. She did not approve of my plan to drive out west on my own, though. I'd saved up money for four years and was undeterred. My boyfriend at the time was a successful musician and maintained a lifestyle I didn't fit into. He was far cooler than me in many ways, and I accepted less respect, attention and care than I deserved because he was a handsome musician. I knew I'd stepped into another sticky relationship trap, or else I'd attracted it. Either way, I preferred to go for a very long drive and try to figure it out before seeing him for a while. Besides, I'd been planning to do this for years and I was finally ready.

I found a house-sitter who'd stay in my apartment, take care of my cat and keep things under control for me. I quit all my jobs knowing I'd start grad school after returning. I had four thousand dollars and four weeks to explore these United States. I talked it over with my cat and she concurred. "Go, explore the world," she purred, "I do it every day, and it's simply marvelous." Nina the shelter cat didn't mind that I talked to my plants and was forever grateful for her freedom. All I had to do was keep the chain lock on my apartment bedroom intact so she could push in and out of it, slink down the fire escape and explore the neighborhood to her heart's content. I insisted she return by nightfall each day, and usually she did. She was the sweetest, most affectionate cat I've ever known, and she shit outside, so no need for a litter box. I wasn't keen on leaving her with someone I didn't know well but was sure she could handle herself as long as he held up his end of the bargain, which he swore he would. Other than paying the rent ahead of time and watering a few plants, I was packed and ready for an adventure I'd spent years dreaming about.

I was on my way, creeping along with Boston traffic when

I experienced a minor fender-bender. No damage, just a wave of apology and a wake-up call that told me, "if you're doing this on your own, you'd better pay attention." So I did. I drove for hours on end, made it to one friend after another, stations of refuge plotted like constellations across the map. I was free to explore. Free to make mistakes and learn from them. Free to get lost and free to find a new way.

As I meandered through the Blue Ridge Mountains, I took time to hike and camp on my own. For some reason, I felt compelled to pick up a hitch-hiker. His name was Sam, and he looked like the nicest grandfather you'd ever meet. He had soft, blue eyes accented with crow's feet and a gentle voice to match. Sam was super grateful I'd stopped and after I dropped him at his destination, he admitted that he needed help the next day as well. If I could pick him up at that same spot near the campground, it would help him complete the entire Appalachian Trail on his own. He'd been hiking it on and off for years with the goal of completing the entire trek. I gave him an easy yes and told him I'd see him in the morning before I retired to my campsite.

As I lay in my tent listening to the sounds of the forest, my mind took a deep dive into the frightening possibilities my mom had warned me about and feared I would encounter. "Don't go into the bayou in the Deep South," she pleaded, "your body will never be found." I waved off her fears like a bad smell but that night they crept into my tent uninvited. I'm a young woman sleeping alone in a tent in the forest several states away from my home. No one knows where I am right now. Was I just playing it cool with Sam? How will I know if I'm really safe? I wondered if I could be savvy enough to stay safe on this solo journey across the country and maintain my faith in humanity simultaneously. The earth beneath my sleeping bag felt comforting and eventually I drifted off to sleep lulled by the gentle sounds of the wilderness surrounding me. It was almost as if my mother's concerns became Mother Earth herself, supporting me every step of the way, and the forest gave me guidance while I slept.

That night I dreamt that I crept from my tent in the middle of the night to sneak to the bathroom not far from my site. It was dark and very foggy. The forest's trees towered above me. I took each step with heightened awareness until I heard a branch snap and froze. Directly ahead of me was a coyote or maybe a wolf. It glared at me, clearly hungry and ready to pounce. At that moment, I knew I was in serious danger. I was the meal, and I had to think of something quick if I wanted to survive. I grabbed a cooking pot from a picnic table and started banging away on it until the wolf's expression turned to one of confusion, and it ran. I made it to the bathroom and looked into the mirror. It was me, but I was different, older, somehow, like I was facing future me.

When I woke up the next day, packed up camp, and began loading the car, fearful thoughts returned. I again wondered if I'd be safe with Sam. Was he genuine? Someone I could trust? Just then, a butterfly landed on my suitcase and I sensed a deep sense of peace and serenity in that moment. This deep feeling of safety and peace was demonstrated by the butterfly's trust that it could rest easy with me for a while. It stayed alight on the handle of my luggage for several minutes, stretching its wings in the morning sun.

Suddenly, the dream I'd had the night before came back to me. The wolf! The dream was guidance: when you're in danger, you'll know it. Trust your instincts to guide you and everything will be okay. The contrast between the gentle, joyful butterfly and fierceness of the wolf made it clear. I realized that Sam was not a threat, but a man who was so close to reaching his goal and in need of a lift. And I could be the one to help him do it. If "hope is the thing with feathers," then joy is a thing with wings. Sam and I met up that morning with equal parts anticipation and gratitude, hope and joy. I dropped him at the trailhead, ready to begin the last of his two-thousand mile hike, and he did it with my help. That experience filled me with confidence for the rest of the trip ahead and gave me courage to help others even if I was afraid.

During the early days of Covid-19, so many people were afraid and didn't know who they could trust. Were the doctors and scientists correct or were they manipulated by pharmaceutical companies driven by greed? I continued to trust my instincts and the need to be of service. Several weeks had passed since the pandemic took control of our everyday lives in March of 2020. Much of this time was spent in denial, just waiting for someone to tell us, "It's all okay now," "It's safe," or "Life can go back to normal." Little did we know that years later we would still be dealing with the impact of this pandemic. In the beginning, though, it was easy to feel totally helpless, locked up at home and afraid to go out. A deep need in me to do something, to be helpful, prompted me to borrow a sewing machine from the rural school district where I teach art.

Delivering homemade face masks to people who needed them deepened my roots here in New York's Southern Tier, where my grandfather came to farm from Germany and where my grandmother raised her five children and put herself through nursing school. Velma, my gram, became one of the few nurses in the area back in the 1950's. She made house calls, treated everything from colds and influenza to broken arms and knife wounds. While

hospitals across the nation scrambled for PPE and pleaded for ventilators to help thousands of people stay alive, brand new sewing machines and 3-D printers, shiny and new, sat silently in our school building just a few miles away. This injustice kept me awake at night. My gram would not have approved of this, and I knew she was cheering on my intention to help others from the Great Beyond.

I had some experience with 3D printers, but the technology education teachers, thinking like I was, started using them to create face shields for healthcare workers. I did not know how to use a sewing machine, but I had plenty of time to learn. My principal, Sara, gave me permission to take one home from school, along with some fabric and thread.

The first day, I broke two steel sewing machine needles, produced a plethora of birds' nests, and finally made two janky face masks in about six hours-time. With some persistence, I solved some common sewing machine conundrums so I could keep the sleek new machine humming long enough to start producing more masks.

The next day, I made my fiftieth face covering and mailed them, so I didn't have to spend an hour getting lost in Allegany County again. A bright red Prius makes a mighty fine target on dirt roads displaying confederate flags and Trump 2020 signs spray- painted on trailers. I didn't truly feel afraid, to be honest. I felt brave. I felt triumphant. I felt more connected with everyone I left with a face mask, regardless of politics.

Popping masks into mailboxes and leaving them on porches was worth a bit of anxiety about getting lost out in the country or stared at by strangers. At this time there were no gloves, no hand sanitizer, no face masks or Personal Protective Equipment to speak of. Medical professionals were required to ration all these things to get through their work day in hospitals, doctors' offices and nursing homes. We made our own hand sanitizer with aloe vera and alcohol. Ada and I figured out how to sew well enough to make face masks, and it felt good to do something positive. Leaving a mask in a sandwich baggie with a note that read, "We love you, we miss you, stay safe," felt more like fifty hugs I wasn't able to give, or fifty laughs no one could hear, or fifty doors held open for whoever is crossing your path; the small gestures of kindness I miss so much about our lives before. That's the norm I miss in normal. It's the "-al" ending, or mostly all of normal I could do without.

By this I mean, the rest of normal: The All-Important Economy. The Bureaucratic Red Tape. The Political Parties. The Glass Ceiling. The Rich Getting Richer. The Sarcasm. Constant opinions spread around like sticky jam. Government Corruption. The Lies. The Entertainment of Exploitation. Domestic Servitude. The Objectification and Disrespect of Girls and Women. The Dying Planet. The Daily Commute. The Daily Grind. Another Species Extinct. Homelessness. Generational Poverty. Racism, Sexism, Ageism. Misinformation. There's a whole lot of "normal" I wish we'd actively and intentionally leave behind. We could abandon most of these things if we truly wanted to.

We had this enormous opportunity at the time to learn some major life lessons together. With so many of us staying indoors, we've noticed wildlife slowly emerge into what seem like safer, quieter spaces. We are part of nature. I see you and recognize your beauty and power in just being you. Interconnection. Interdependence. Kinship. Humanity. Loving-Kindness. Will we deepen our compassion enough to learn some of these lessons? So many of us seem to miss all parts of the normal way of life before Covid-19. They'd likely embrace all of it and make excuses for the destructive parts just to have their routines and paychecks back on track, money flowing in rather than out. I do understand the desperation and anxiety poverty produces, so this is understandable. People need paychecks. I just wish they didn't cost us so much of our humanity.

Kind gestures are valuable outputs that bring a natural return. You get what you give. So, I'll keep feeding the squirrels and birds. I'll keep making masks for anyone who tells me they want one, and maybe for a few who don't. You never know where seeds like these will land or how they might take root, what they might look like when a few of them eventually blossom on a rainy April day. And someone, coasting along, will notice them and smile.

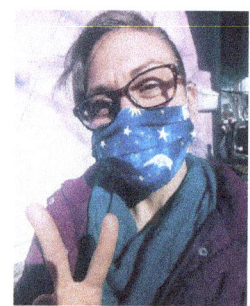

Like Mother, Like Daughter

"People who live in glass houses should not throw stones."
— Chinese Proverb (and my mom)

Ada's hair has never been so long. It's practically to her hips now, ranging from a tawny, golden brown at the roots to a sunset yellow-like straw at the ends; and tangled like you wouldn't believe. I long to brush it, but it hurts her, so I ask her to brush it out on her own instead. Then I play with it gently, give it a braid or two, and imagine what it will look like after we donate to "Locks for Love," which is a thrilling fantasy of mine after her bald baby head grew nothing but soft fuzz for the first two years of her life. My hair, on the other hand, grows more out than down. I have a thick wave of maple-brown tendrils that seem to grow around and through, like roots navigating rocks in soil. More of these tendril-hairs have given up their pigment and shine like mirrors now, a bright grandmotherly white. I like the white hairs and secretly wish for more to fill in like streaks of lightning. When we play with one another's hair, it feels like everything's going to be alright.

Yet, as I brush through the thin layer that is left of my mother's hair, I feel a deep sadness. During a weekend visit to see my mom, I use the round bristle brush she's always used on her hair but can no longer muster the strength to wield. Mom's Parkinson's disease is eating away at her mind-body slowly, like a giant slug feasting on a vegetarian buffet. She has less connection to her body, less access to her own emotions, and more frustration arising in the struggle for everyday tasks, or ADLs, as they call them. The Activities of Daily Living we take for granted. Brushing your hair, your teeth, pulling on socks, tying shoelaces, dressing, fastening your seatbelt, walking across the kitchen, using the bathroom. So many of these activities seem like Olympic events for her now. So, I focus on her hair. I tell her it looks lovely today. I hand her a mirror to look at it, and she thanks me. I see you, mom, and I love you. In spite of everything, I love you. I think these things silently since we do not have the ability or the trust required in our relationship to name or share feelings.

My visit to Cortland County was abrupt and unplanned. My mom called to let me know, only because her boyfriend of ten years, Evan, said he would tell me if she didn't. Through tears, she carefully unraveled her story: "I woke up early and wanted to go for a drive. So, I went to see my sister, Janie. Well, I got a bit lost driving around her neighborhood. All the houses looked the same at night. It was so dark. I wasn't sure where I was, but I knew I was close enough... So, I parked the car and walked around until I found her house. I knocked on the door, but she wouldn't answer. I guess it was very early, maybe two or two-thirty in the morning. Well, Janie got scared and called the police. A very nice officer showed up, and he was very helpful. I explained that this was my sister's house, so he called her, and she came to the door finally. It all worked out, and I stayed the rest of the night there.

I called Evan in the morning, and he and Grace came to get me…" And then, in a strained whisper, she said, "That's when they took my keys." This was difficult for her to tell me, and she wouldn't have without Evan's threat to tell it himself. "Mom," I asked, "why did you go out for a drive in the middle of the night?" She didn't know. She was still angry and upset about not being able to drive her "own, damn car." I tried to reassure her. "They just want you to be safe, that's all, mom." It was clear to me that Parkinson's just won a small victory, and I needed to go support her.

Undeterred by the pandemic, and ignoring state-wide "stay-at-home" orders, I went anyway. This was an emergency. I wanted my mom to know that I would be there for her, no matter what. This was long before any vaccines were invented for Covid-19, and I knew it was a risk. It takes more than three hours to arrive at their farm, so I didn't visit very often. Mom had stopped wanting to drive long distances herself a few years ago. I remembered this and planned out a few reasons why not driving anymore was going to be okay.

When I arrived, I reassured her that not driving for a while was for the best, and that it was just for now, and that Evan would take her anywhere she wanted to go. "I know he will," she said, as her trembling hands fumbled with a zipper. I leaned in and asked, "do you want help with that?" With her head hanging down, she whispered, "Yes, thank you." It was during this visit when she first told me about the hallucinations.

"Just look at this," she said, as she led me into her bedroom. We were standing near a window, blinds drawn, looking at the side of the bed. I looked but only saw folds in the blanket of a hastily made bed. "Is it this?" I asked, smoothing the folds out with both hands. "Oh, well now it's gone," she said with a hint of disappointment. "What's gone?" I asked. "The faces. See, now there's another one there," she pointed to the top corner of the room, in front of a sweater hanging on the back of the door. "I don't see anything, mom. Is it a face you recognize? Is it a person you know?" "Well, I think it's the founder of the farm, the one who started this place." She proceeded to take me on a tour of the numerous faces hovering in different parts of the bedroom, including the closet where the bifold doors stood open, revealing their presence. "I think these may be memories, mom. Maybe your brain is showing you all the people you remember seeing in the past."

I didn't know if that was true. I only knew that some of the Big Pharma medicine she was taking gave her some serious side-effects, and I was there to comfort her, not analyze the medications. Later I learned that visual and auditory hallucinations are a common phase Parkinson's patients endure. My mom continues to see people who are not there in the physical world, and she admits that she can't tell what's real and what's not. It's all very real to her, and as she always used to say, "People who live in glass houses should not throw stones."

We all live in some sort of glass box. We think it's safe. We think it's home, but it can shatter at any moment from words, lies, or stones. We moved so many times while I was growing up there are some "homes" I don't even remember. Most of the homes were not homes at all, just temporary shelter. For me, this whole idea of a home became very separated from the place you live. My mom was my home. When I left for college she reminded me, "your home is with me for as long as you want it."

She always liked getting her hair cut and styled, so during this visit, I did my best with a dampened brush and a few sincere compliments. She seemed to brighten temporarily, like sunshine briefly revealed behind racing clouds. I noticed her shuffling feet and slanted stance, wincing, as Parkinson's pulled her down slowly. I watched her take thirty minutes to make a sandwich with bread, cheese, and a slice of turkey, without even a thought of making a meal for the rest of the family, as if such a task had become an athletic event she hadn't registered for in years.

I made some food and cleaned out the fridge, cleaned here and there, did some raking in the yard, planted a rose bush, and laid out some mulch. She sat her frail body in a folding chair that looked like it could swallow her whole, as she helped with a smaller rake and bag by her side. She marveled at all the work we completed and thanked me up and down. The setting sun shone orange on our work, like a spotlight at the closing of a play.

After I returned home, I called the Office of the Aging for Cortland County every other day for a month to get some basic services set up for her. I shared my observations and got her on a list. I begged and pleaded and got more names and numbers. I thanked and complemented anyone willing to listen to me. All services, especially for the elderly, the most vulnerable among us, have been severely cut back during the pandemic. It was nearly impossible to get anyone on the phone who might be able to connect you with any in-person services. Finally, we had Meals on Wheels delivered to her once a week. Just a pair of eyes on her shuffling to the door would give me some reassurance. It would be someone checking on her regularly. "Wouldn't it be nice to not have to cook dinner once a week, mom?" I asked, thrilled at the idea myself. One meal from the Wheels. That's all she took. "It was cold, canned vegetables, Kristin. I told them not to come back."

Ten months later, my mom's Parkinson's disease was ravaging her body like a jealous lover, curving her spine laterally, as her left leg shook uncontrollably with spasms. The medicine helped some, but wreaked havoc on her body with side-effects almost as bad as the symptoms they were meant to control. I'd shown her videos of a man suffering with similar Parkinson's symptoms and how quick and effective cannabis oil was at treating the muscular shaking. I had oil I could give her. My friend Jen made it for her friend who suffered from multiple sclerosis. This became part of her treatment that helped keep her symptoms at bay. I was hoping it might do the same for my mom. "I can give you some to try," I said, with a bit too much hope in my voice. "Oh, Evan would throw it out if he found out."

Later, red-faced and angry, Evan called me a drug dealer for even considering such alternatives. So, we continued to watch her take twenty different medications from little orange bottles that caused a need for more medications. Helping nothing but her addiction to medications, her disease worsened. Early one morning, my mom fell in the kitchen and broke her left hip.

When I close my eyes and think about how it must have happened, I see it in slow motion, with her hip shattering as her side hit the floor at the first moment of impact, a stunned look on her face, unaware of how the floor had jumped up so suddenly. Emergency hip surgery was performed to repair the damage, and we were hopeful she would be discharged in a few days.

Three months passed. My mom could not be discharged from the hospital because she was not standing or walking independently, she had a high risk of falling and needed around the clock care. She received physical therapy in the hospital, which was helping, but hospital restrictions banning visitations helped to sharpen the hallucinations, allowing her to reject reality and give in to another world entirely. In her mind, she was writing plays and directing them too. She worked with all kinds of children and was being given an award for her work. All from a hospital bed, without any technology or even the ability to answer a ringing telephone. Nurses needed to go into her room and answer the phone for her if you wanted to get through and speak to her over the phone. She missed being around family, but other than that she seemed quite content working on her "screenplays," and watching the films in her mind, ones that acknowledged her sacrifice, her work, and thanked her for it.

One of my mother's favorite phrases was always, "don't look a gift horse in the mouth," as we rolled our eyes at the orange in the toe of the Christmas stocking, or underwear as a gift for any occasion. She explained the phrase a few times, for added effect. "If someone gives you a horse, you can bet it's a pretty old one, and so you'd look at its teeth to see just how old that horse might be. Instead, just be grateful someone's giving you anything at all!" she'd say, shaking her finger at me.

I was grateful. I was aware that she'd made a big sacrifice, going back to school as a single parent, being paid far less than her worth and far less than most men in business. I could see she was stressed most of the time. She'd come home after six p.m. exhausted and make us dinner. She yelled a lot, and daily. She would get red in the face and scream and slam cupboards and doors when I said the wrong thing or question why I had to empty the dishwasher when Freddy never did. She had a quick temper, little patience, and high blood pressure. I became attuned to her blood pressure because it helped to know when a pot was going to boil over so you could get out of the way. I learned how to hide in a closet fort and cry in silence. Instead of feeling loved and cherished, I felt like a burden throughout my childhood.

My mom may have wanted to maintain custody of her kids through the divorce, but she couldn't handle the responsibility on her own. I think she missed our father and regretted cheating on him, but she never said so. She never learned how to manage stress, communicate her feelings appropriately, or use any kind of self-care to cope with the dynamic nature of life. She just yelled and slammed doors and let her blood pressure skyrocket. I felt so sad for her. If I asked her how she was, she most often replied, "miserable." As a kid, that is how it felt to be around her much of the time.

There were times she would laugh or relax enough to enjoy someone else's company, but more often than not, she suffered from stress and physical ailments. Migraines, allergies, sinusitis, sinus headaches, high blood pressure, constipation, menstrual cramps, heavy bleeding and cysts that led to a full hysterectomy at the age of forty. Later, a lump in her breast led to minor surgery to remove it and I changed her bandages and cleaned the wound for three or four days. I was always there to take care of things—to turn off all the lights, to bring her pills, to answer the phone, make dinner, clean the dishes and the kitchen, walk the dog, or to just keep quiet. I became a very good codependent from my mom's addiction to anger and prescription medication. It was a volatile combination, so I did whatever she wanted, as soon as instructed to avoid "the Hulk," as we called her. She would suddenly transform like Dr. Bruce Banner, a decent, hard-working person, into a green monstrosity full of jealousy, anger, and rageful energy.

One night, when I was in high school and had a pile of homework to complete, my mom was out late. She may have had a conference or a meeting after work and came home unusually late. She had no doubt expected the house to be quiet, for no kids to be up, and to have the place to herself. When she saw me still up at the kitchen table doing homework, she transformed. Rage took over her body and she shrieked, "What are you still doing up?" as she used the three-ring binders and clipboard in her hands to bash me over the head repeatedly. I tried to block her blows with my arms, but they just kept coming, and she just kept shrieking, "What-are-you-still-doing-up?" landing another blow with each word. I was in shock and curled into a defensive position, protecting my head instinctively.

Finally, Freddy stepped in. He was a senior in high school then and had never stood up for me before. He pulled the Hulk off me, yelling, "Mom, stop!" and she stormed upstairs, slamming her bedroom door. This didn't happen often, but her rage was ever-present, just below the skin, ready for transformation. I loved her in spite of these violent outbursts. And so did Evan, dairy farmer and classmate from Homer High School. Evan loved my mom, but he was stubborn as a mule.

Evan wanted her to return home from the hospital as soon as possible, but I wasn't sure that was the best idea. When I see how dependent my mom is on others, how frail and frustrated she seems, I remind myself that this is all our fate. Buddha taught the simple truth that suffering exists in the world. We will all grow old, get sick, and die, in our own special ways, of course, in our own screenplays. When we recognize suffering in all its many forms, and accept it as an integral part of life, we can ignite compassion for others. In fact, when compassion is truly alive inside us, we do not look upon others as others, instead we see ourselves.

My mom's misery showed me how not to live. Her anger, stress, and unhappiness created a clear picture of how not to be an adult. When I grew up, all I knew was that I wanted to be happy. Yoga, meditation, time in nature, music, dancing, art, and all kinds of creativity and adventure were ways for me to discover self-care and stress management, but these were also pathways to experience gratitude, wonder, and joy. Every time I found something I enjoyed, I made a point to practice it, to be with it longer. My mom appreciated my drawing skills and saw that I enjoyed the arts. She always hung up my artwork in the hallway of any apartment we lived in and kept stacks of my drawings and writing in a hope chest at the foot of her bed. She encouraged me to attend art school and do something I loved. Another one of her favorite phrases was, "Do as I say, not as I do," because she didn't want me to be like her either.

I believe that her deepest regret was not making amends with my father, for their divorce, and for having betrayed his trust. These things could never be fixed. She could not undo her affair, her lies, or cheating. She could not undo the yelling or screaming, she could only move forward. I believe she kept moving us as kids, because as soon as she felt settled, at home once again, she'd start longing for my dad, to have him there with us, and she had to start planning the next move as a distraction from her grief and pain. No matter how different my mom and I seem to be today, I know the truth is, "Like mother, like daughter." My heart was also broken when they divorced. We lost the same man in different ways. I too have to keep moving my body or working with my hands in order to think or find some measure of peace inside. I've learned to sit with discomfort and pain, however. I watch it pass, sometimes roughly, like an ocean wave, sometimes gently, like how a rainbow fades. Either way, if you can learn to witness your own feelings, to experience your own pain, it always transforms.

I had many more opportunities to learn, grow, try new things, and make a better life for myself, mostly because of my mother's sacrifices. If I'd stayed in a loveless marriage, I would no doubt be a stressed-out hulk of a human too. It seemed that my mom became this after leaving her marriage, which never brought her the happiness she sought. Happiness, of course, is an inside job. Shifting your perspective until you have what you want and want what you have, with a sense of gratitude brings a deep contentment. Focusing on gratitude always brings me peace. This may sound odd, but I'm grateful for my mom's Parkinson's disease.

She no longer has high blood pressure. She's calm and doesn't have the ability to express violent rage anymore. She doesn't have a shopping bag full of prescription drugs to take anymore, just the Parkinson's medicine. She's found a different dimension that interests her much more than this one, and she dives into it. During one visit she told me she had a new job working for the Lion Tamer that ran the circus, and she was his assistant. She was the one who stuck her head into the lion's mouth during the show! "Wow, mom! That's incredible and very brave. I'm impressed!" I shared as sincerely as I could. Quite often she would tell me about her newest job. Sometimes it was writing screenplays, or working with kids, sometimes it was working with animals. I think these were things she dreamt of doing in this life but never had the opportunity. With these fantastic new dimensions of work and life, she spends most of her time imagining, wondering, and drifting off to sleep. When I see her, I bring lotion to rub into her long, bony fingers, file her nails, and brush her hair. I ask her if she remembers when we went to Myrtle Beach and she forgot her suitcase, which I know she does. "I swore up and down that one of you kids took it," she'd say, as she slapped her thigh, doubling over with laughter. We have a nice chuckle looking back through the tunnel of time. When I finish her hair and say, "There! You're a beauty." She chuckles out loud and I smile.

After returning home to the Pink House, relieved to be with my loves once again, I found this poem I'd written twenty-five years ago. I wrote it for my mom's birthday when I lived in Boston, in a whole different life and only saw my mom once or twice a year. Of course, I never shared it with her.

The First Person I Can Remember
Not only because
I too am guilty
of forgetting your birthday,
but because
so much has disappeared
between us since I've been here.
It's become easier to rush in and out,
to phone once a week
or not at all.
It's gotten easier to eat standing up and
on my way out the door.
Back in our little apartment across

from the high school,
we moved in and
You made it look like a home
before noon the next day,
hanging pictures on the walls as I got up
for breakfast.
I remember you.
Even back as far as
sitting on your lap.
You and gram both gave me that comfort
for as long as you could.
I used to try to match my breathing
to yours exactly,
While there on your lap.
New shoes and boots and warm coats
each winter season,
the socks and sweaters and
brown paper packages sent through the mail,
Our phone calls back and forth, messages left like
bits of color in my hair.
None should have been left without a Thank you, or
I love you, or Take care, and
on your one day
every feeling should be sent to celebrate the fact
that you are here.
I remember you.
Your sighs, and
Sounds of running bathwater
sent me off into the night.

Always with a kiss.
Your weary shoulders after quite a day.
"Oh, miserable,...horrible," you would say
with a smile.
I cannot leave the miserable days behind,
they will always reappear.
I cannot call everyday or sit down to eat at six.
But I can sigh like you do, and
breathe deeply at least,
and sip my tea.
and know quite positively
that you are the first person I can remember.

March 25th, 1995

Tea Bag Wisdom

"When there is Love there are no questions."
— Yogi Tea (from the Yoga Sutras)

S hakta, our yoga teacher, gave us our first assignment for the retreat: Bring a game, a story, or an activity of some sort to share with the group after lunchtime. It was only our second day together at the retreat in the wilderness of West Virginia. There were twelve of us, plus a vegan chef who looked like a Brazilian goddess, an Indian yoga teacher named Jyoti, Shakta, and occasionally, her husband Kartar, both former students of the late Yogi Bhajan who formed this new tribe I had paid a lot of money to join. I immediately humiliated myself by crying during my introduction the day before and explained that I was going through a painful divorce and to forgive me for being so sad. I don't recall what it was I said, honestly, just the feeling of dread and embarrassment I was left with. I do remember, however, the following group share: specifically, the tea-bag reading activity.

We chose a bag of tea with inspirational messages printed on their little paper tags. We first had to think of a question we wanted answered. We talked about all the questions we have about our lives, our futures, and sat for a few moments in meditation before choosing a tea bag and read it to ourselves silently. We shared around the circle what we thought our message meant. Mine read, "Where there is love, there are no questions." Really? All I had were questions:

Why can't he keep a reliable job?

Why won't he start going back to AA meetings again, even just once a month?

Why don't we connect or have intimate moments anymore?

Why doesn't he want to spend time with me and his daughter?

Why are we not enough: entertaining enough, loving enough, exciting enough, etc., for him to put us first, just once? Or once in a while?

Why won't he go for walks with me? Take us out for a picnic? A bike ride?

Why do I have to negotiate spending time with him?

Why won't he help out around the house without being asked or begged?

Why do I have to do everything on my own?

Why do I have to work all the time, pay most of the bills, and come home and cook dinner or shovel sidewalks before I leave for work in the morning?

Why do I have to be in tears for him to truly listen to anything I have to say?

What kind of marriage is this I'm in?

When was the last time we had sex?

How can he afford $65 golf pants with paisley prints all over them when he has debtors calling him weekly and steep loans to pay off?

Why does his kindness or help always have an invisible string attached?

Why does his rage come out so easily when I want to talk about our relationship? Why do I feel invisible in my own life?

All I had were unanswered questions. This tea bag game offered no solutions, just cryptic symbols, certainly no real answers. I wanted an answer to each one of these questions, honest answers, from my husband. "When there is love there are no questions?" So, if I loved him, I wouldn't question how I was regarded in our marriage? Fucking bullshit, man. I tucked it into a journal and left it, exhausted after more shared activities, yoga classes, lectures, and chores. That night I didn't sleep and got up from the lower bunk I was calling home for the next two weeks and dragged myself to one of the long, textured couches in the expansive living room space we used for classes. Large salt lamps kept a warm, steady glow there all the time, and I liked it, even though it didn't help me sleep. It did, however, present me with yet another question: How the hell did I get here?

Five-thirty a.m. yoga class followed by seven a.m. break-fast, without coffee was the next day's punishment for not getting the tea bag saying. But this, this was my goal, getting my Yoga Teacher Certification was my thing, and I was making it happen, no matter what. This was it, the end of the steady stream of hours and credit card transactions, aside from finding a mentor and documenting my initial teaching back home, I really was almost there. Eventually I must have detoxed from caffeine and sugar, adjusted to the early morning classes and late-night chores. I learned the lay of the land walking the grounds of the retreat center as well as who I could talk to, who I could confide in. The discipline of early to bed and early to rise, practicing yoga and meditation every day was beginning to feel…good. It began to feel like answers were forming. The answers, I would find later, were not the ones I was hoping for.

I was getting to know other people in meaningful ways, however. Bridget, a special education teacher, left her job with a school district to homeschool her twins and start her own yoga studio. Nazira, a beautiful Russian woman, took strong medication for intimate problems and felt trapped in an emotionally abusive triangle with her husband and his mother. Sophia, a powerfully grounded and physically strong woman from Colorado was just as flat-chested as I am but had confidence and self-love. She was a counselor who used yoga and mindfulness in her practice. All these women helped me begin to see that I have a story too. That I have a history as well as a future, and this retreat was the opportunity we all needed to pivot on our paths, just a bit.

The next five-thirty a.m. yoga class followed by seven a.m. breakfast without coffee was the next day's labor for still not getting the tea bag saying. Soon after the morning's practice, I noticed some of my stubborn grumpiness and anger soften enough to relax a little, to notice and appreciate the people around me. Once again, we sat on the floor of the large, open living room space preparing for a lecture when someone jumped up and out of the way of a small creature. It was a large wolf spider, a mother, like many of us there in that space. She moved slowly, but confidently toward the open glass doors. When I leaned in enough to see her up close, I realized she was carrying a voluminous sack of eggs on her back. Any arachnophobia I had quickly vanished. Was it heavy? Was she afraid? Did she know where to go to keep her babies safe? A sea of yoga mats and cushions parted for her silently as she made her way toward the cool breeze of wilderness beyond the glass doors. Good luck mama, I whispered, and suddenly, I understood.

When true, abiding love exists in the heart, the questions that carry our doubt, fear, and worry, simply do not arise. When you are in the presence of real love, you have no need for combative or comparative queries like I had. When you are filled with gratitude, peace, and love for yourself and others, questions are born of curiosity, not criticism. "Where there is love, there are no questions" simply meant that my marriage was indeed without the presence of love, and deep down, I knew this. The sheer weight and nature of my questions showed that love was no longer present between us. This was beginning to make sense, but I had to be sure this was it.

Later that evening we were granted some free time to do as we pleased, so I called my husband. He knew that I was unhappy in our marriage and that I was looking for more. I'd let him in on my feelings of discontent before leaving for Virginia and promised to let him know what I wanted to do after I returned from the retreat. Out of curiosity, I asked him what it was that he wanted to happen between us. He said quite simply, "I want to live in our house and be with Ada," (our four-year-old daughter.) It occurred to me that I had no place in this plan, that I was not even a part of what he wanted. "That's exactly what it feels like," I said. I felt invisible, and it hurt. No matter how many questions I posed to him, he had reasons, logical answers and often criticism, but it did not feel loving anymore. It was this moment on the telephone that confirmed a new direction on my own path, a pivot. It helped me move a little further along, but in a new direction…toward the fresh breeze coming from the wilderness beyond the glass, just like mama spider. "Where there is love there are no questions." I finally got it.

I refused to live a life without love or stay in a marriage that was loveless.

Once I see something clearly, I can't unsee it. Eventually, I would learn that love does not require two people. Once I decided to focus all my energy on healing my heart and pouring my loving attention into myself, my daughter, and my life, I found a deeper, truer sense of love that had been there all along. I discovered that I loved my life. I loved myself. I loved Ada. Being free, finally, from bargaining and begging for love from someone who did not have it to give allowed me to realize the love I already had but was not fully embracing. In time, I began to love, and live again, in a whole new direction.

Take Me Home

"Well, I've been a prisoner all my life, and I can say to you, but I don't remember." — Phil Collins

There was an old farmhouse built on a stone foundation with a dirt cellar. It had a covered porch out front and sat dangerously inside the elbow of a hairpin curve along Route 64. My bedroom was just above the porch, and my mom had a deep fear that one night, while I was asleep in my bed, a driver would speed around the hairpin turn and take out the posts holding up our porch and my bedroom would come crashing down with it. As a four-year-old, I was aware of my mom's fear, and every night I went to bed, I said my prayers. "Now I lay me down to sleep, I pray the Lord my soul to keep, If I should die before I wake, I pray the Lord my soul to take." This prayer still gives me the creeps. Why would you want your child to think about death right before going to sleep over a porch that hung dangerously close to a hairpin curve? I mean, good grief.

In the first grade we learned all about dinosaurs and one night before bed, it dawned on me that all the dinosaurs are gone. They died. They didn't come back after they died. When you die, you don't come back. You're gone forever. I sobbed uncontrollably and my mom rubbed my back as she sat on the side of my bed. I thought of my cousin Kristy, and my grandfather, and all the dinosaurs and continued to sob. My brother came in and asked, "What's the matter with her?" My mom just shrugged her shoulders and kept rubbing my back in circles. I didn't know how to explain that this new understanding filled my entire being with dread. Every night since then, I have been hyper aware of my own mortality and remember it as I slip into the darkened quiet of sleep. My heart races, my breathing becomes shallow, and I dive into what could be the void of the Great Beyond. The place no one talks about, especially with kids.

Every memory I have from living with my parents in the farmhouse is crystal clear and colorful. One summer afternoon, I meandered down the grassy path toward our pond, singing to the birds as I went. The birds seemed to recognize me, chattered back to me, like they accepted me as one of their own. Like they knew me. The wild grasses were taller than I was and moved like slow dancers in the wind. I took each step with purpose and curiosity. I was one with nature, in perfect harmony, and totally free. I would sneak down to the pond hoping to see a turtle or frog along its edge. I remember the sun on our white rowboat, upside down near a large rock on the bank of the pond. I peeked out through the cattails to see a Great Blue Heron on the opposite side of the pond. It was the most magical creature I'd ever laid eyes on. It was standing on some low branches close to the water, and it saw me too. That moment is still with me today.

Hearing my mother call for me, I ran back to the house and plopped down beneath the great willow tree in the backyard. Our black cat, Mittens, climbed onto my lap purring. Snapdragons in every color lined the edges of the vegetable garden. I helped my dad plant rows and rows of corn, puzzled why the corn kernels were blue. "It's fertilizer," he'd explain, and go on and on about what the plant needed to be healthy. I felt the sun and the breeze just as I felt the safety of my parents sharing a home together. One autumn day I was standing at the living room window gasping in wonder at the orange and yellow leaves falling from the sky, the wind painting motion pictures for my enjoyment. My dad was frying bologna in a pan, watching a big bubble of hot air form in the middle, like a hungry tummy waiting for breakfast. I carry these memories with me still, like a photo album in my mind, but they are photos I can smell and taste and touch.

There was a large barn painted a lovely butter yellow, with pens for pigs. Pinky and Stinky were the names of our two plump piglets. I loved them so. My brother and I would go out and talk to them while they snorted about in their pens alongside the yellow barn. I thought my pig, Pinky, was the loveliest and sweetest of all pigs, and that her name suited her perfectly. My big brother Freddy's pig was gross. He was a muddy gray color and loved rolling in the mud. I loved Stinky too, but I pretended not to. One morning at the farmhouse, there was talk of bacon for breakfast. I skipped into the mudroom as my dad opened the freezer revealing packages wrapped in white butcher paper. "Thanks to Pinky and Stinky," he said, "We have plenty of bacon." I couldn't believe it at first, but realized that indeed, my beloved pigs were gone, and our freezer was full. This stirred a deep disturbance in me

I struggle to articulate to this day. Nausea comes close, and vegetarianism soon after. I haven't eaten a piece of pork or red meat in decades. Just the thought of it takes me back to that spot in the mudroom, heartbroken and betrayed.

The old farmhouse seemed to have hundreds of doors. One at each end of the staircase, one at every room, and extras everywhere. Maybe this helped keep the warmth inside the few occupied rooms, or maybe it was for exclamation in an argument, or to run and hide behind after you discover your parents slaughtered your beloved pets for food. I heard more and more doors slam shut, muffled arguments, my mom's red face and bloodshot eyes. One afternoon mom sat me and Freddy down on the floor in the living room because she had something to tell us. "Your dad and I are getting a divorce," she said. I didn't know this word and tilted my head to one side as I caught a glimpse of my big brother's face all screwed up, eyes squeezed shut, tears leaking out. He began to cry, and therefore, so did I. Whatever this means, it's bad, I thought.

I could not understand why the grown-ups worked so hard and spent so much time working on the house, fixing it up just to sell it to somebody else. If you don't want it, why are you taking such good care of it, giving it so much of your time and attention? Everything seemed upside down, and soon after that, my mom moved us into an apartment. Not just one apartment, but ten. Every year, there would be a better apartment, or a little yard space, or cheaper rent, or one that accepted pets. We moved so many times that I didn't bother telling my father our new address, knowing it would just change again in a minute. My mom was terrible at talking to us kids, at explaining all the changes, so she bought us gifts instead. A Walkman, a stuffed animal, candy, a new blanket. When the gifts were presented for no apparent reason, Freddy and I would shoot each other a sideways glance and understand that it meant we were moving again.

My mom was good at unpacking, hanging pictures and setting up a home. She reminded me of Suzy squirrel tidying up her little home way up high in the old oak tree, dusting her shelves and wiping down her acorn cups. It was my mom's way of beginning again and simultaneously avoiding looking back or inward. It was this repetitive futility that illustrated how personal happiness is an inside job, that, wherever you go, there you are. It matters little what kind of house you live in, or what things you own—we can be perfectly miserable surrounded with luxury. Happiness comes from giving time and attention to your heart's still, small voice inside. Often, it's a soft whisper the rest of life drowns out. We can stop and take notice of what's inside, take time to feel gratitude, to make plans you feel dedicated to seeing through, not to avoid life, but to embrace it. This, not a new home, is where happiness originates. Growing up, I dreamed of my life back at the farmhouse, my pond and Willow tree, and longed for it, longed for time in the garden with my father again, until I cried myself to sleep before slipping into the darkness once again. I was deeply unhappy with this new life without my father. And my mom, my mom was miserable too.

Steadily hard-working, my mom supported us through her full-time job with Eastman Kodak and later, GE Capital. She wore nylon stockings and high heeled shoes every workday. She came home after six or six thirty every night, exhausted and stressed, angry that more work awaited her at home. I grew to feel like a burden, a heavy load on her back. My mom's worries became my own. I worried about money and tried not to ask for anything, but mom found ways to get us new coats, shoes, and school clothes every year.

Her blood pressure was high, and I became attuned to it, when she yelled and swore things like, "Shut the G.D. door!" or "Pick your clothes up off the floor for God's sake!" When she drove like a drag car racer, swearing at other drivers, her blood pressure was high. When my brother and I bickered, her blood pressure was high. Our mom was a stressed out, single parent doing her level best, suffering along a path to nowhere. Only when she slept was her blood pressure normal. She took medication to get it "under control," but that never made any sense to me. If you have to keep taking it, year after year, then it must not be working. The real way to control your blood pressure is to get yourself, and your life, under control, which unfortunately, my mom never learned how to do. She would just make decisions, without anyone else, pack up all our stuff and move us to a new apartment to start over again.

When I graduated from Fairport high school, we were living in the townhouse apartments across the street. I liked walking to school in the morning and going home for lunch in the middle of the day. Back then, Fairport High had two women, both named Carol, who patrolled the hallways for students skipping class or attempting escape. No cameras, just Carols. My mom photocopied one hand-written note that stated, "My daughter, Kristin Buchholz, has my permission to come home from school for lunch today." Signed, Pat Buchholz. There was a large stack of these official notes by the door and every day, I would take one to school and back with me just in case the Carols needed some form of documentation. One day, I forgot the note, but, I reasoned, I'm coming back to school. Why would someone hassle me for returning to a place of learning? The Carols nabbed me without a note and sent me to the principal's office. I remember my hands shaking, I was so nervous. He listened to my explanation, paused, and said, "Don't do it again. You're free to go." Relief flooded my entire body as I raced home, shaking my head at the continued nonsense of adults.

Upon my high school graduation, my mom decided it was time to move again, and she purchased a little house in the city of Rochester. It would be much closer to work for her, and both of us kids would be at college. When I returned home for the first time after my freshman year at Syracuse, it was to a place I'd never been before: cozy and quaint, but utterly foreign. The Norfolk Pine and mother-in-law's tongues still alive and well, same knick-knacks on the shelf above the sofa, so it must be home. I wondered how long my mom would last in this place. Could she actually settle for once and put down some roots? My magic eight ball always said, "Very Doubtful." But we planted perennials, got a dog, fixed up the place, and my mom became Suzy Squirrel again, quite content in her own magical realm. She was good at making any place feel comfortable, familiar—like a home, or at least, her version of what home was supposed to look like. How it sounded and what it felt like were altogether different in my mind.

Rainbow In The Fountain

"Love yourself first and everything else falls into line."
— Lucille Ball

I t had been eleven days since I last saw my daughter, Ada. She was four years old then, and she was perfect. It was the longest day yet, with what felt like a heavy shroud swallowing me slowly, weighing me down. I'd made some new friends at the retreat. Shiny, happy people, all of us completing our Yoga Teacher Training in the wilderness of West Virginia. Yet, my heart ached for her. My husband, my mother, mother-in-law and a few trustworthy neighbors had all been tasked with caring for Ada while I was away.

My goal was to get my 200-hour teacher training certification before I turned forty. I had worked at it for three summers now, and this was day eleven of twelve before I would be, well, not completely done. I would still need to find a mentor, teach classes, and videotape them, and then get feedback from said mentor, take a written exam, and of course, spend more money I didn't have.

I would never be done. On this eleventh day, my heart sank into some dark, internal pit, leaving a handy void in my chest for panic and dread to rush in. I could smell my daughter's hair when I breathed in. I could hear her giggle when I closed my eyes. I could feel her on my lap, tying her miniature shoes, holding her tiny hands. Saving her voicemail messages left for me when I was unable to answer the phone, I would replay them and take in the sweetness of her voice like a drug. I finally let it spill out of me like a guilt-riddled thief. I told my teacher that I had to leave, that I might not be able to make it another day away from her. This felt like actual withdrawal symptoms I could no longer tolerate. The longing on my face was so apparent, she addressed this directly in class. "These are just thoughts. They are not real. And feelings fade… In fact, being fully in the present is exactly how to get somewhere else."

What a perfect teachable moment! She must have thought herself a sage, like Yogi Bhajan himself. To me, her proclamation felt like a surgical knife letting me bleed out. I coasted through the rest of the day like a junkie; strung out, shaking, walking alone, talking to God, begging. All because I missed my beloved daughter so terribly.

Also, because I knew in my heart of hearts that I had to leave my husband. We'd been engaged for four years and married for almost eight. Ada, our one and only, utterly perfect child, was a mere bud on a sapling at four years old. She brought us so much joy, yet rarely together. By that I mean, she brought us joy, separately. Chad and I were rarely together.

As a guileless co-dependent, I was unaware that "Golf-Pro" wasn't a great match for anyone wishing to have a family. It turns out that "Golf-Pro" meant exactly two things: never home. Quite some time after we were married, I discovered and embraced the term "Golf Widow." It was a constant source of contention yet also a sardonic inside joke among family and friends. As a teacher, I had lovely, warm months of the year free to devote to family, to pursuing dreams, adventures, and national parks with loved ones. School vacations and two glorious months of summer healed the stress of the daily grind. As a Golf-Pro, Chad worked those same months like a workaholic; like it was the only time of year he would make money at any significant rate all year long, which it was. So, fourteen hours a day on the golf course was the norm, six or seven days a week.

There were some interesting times when I found myself, baby in tow, picnic lunch ready in the car, at the golf course begging him to spend an hour with us. Nothing but resentments seemed to flow between us. I wanted him to want to be in partnership with me, alongside me with our beautiful daughter. He was not and never would be, it turned out. I didn't know it back then, but I would find a way out of what felt like a long, dark tunnel. How could I put Ada through the pain of her parents divorcing like my parents had done to me? How could I possibly hurt her so deeply?

Driving, walking the dog, or taking a break at school, I would call Alysia in tears. I needed her, and she was always there to listen. "Just keep walking through the fire," she'd say. "You can do this," she'd whisper. She saw me and led me, just like when we were kids, every time I called from the depths of this maze.

There were three or more labyrinths there, on this retreat center property in the wilderness of West Virginia. A labyrinth is a maze that you choose to walk into, hoping for a feasible exit. One maze was lined with crystals and special stones. Another was simpler and held a path of woodchips shaped into an elaborate geometric design. The owner of the property was a middle-aged woman with long, honey-colored hair and sun-kissed skin who was a certified Shaman, and whose sister talks to spirits. You could pay $30 for an appointment with her sister to talk to the spirits who hovered around you, deciphering their messages. On this day, though, I walked the labyrinths again. They were free. The one with giant crystals of quartz and amethyst lining the walkway was my favorite. I had never in my life seen anything quite like it. Quartz the size of boulders, and one with a little wooden house built around it. If you held your hand near this giant quartz, you could feel it vibrating. Amethyst the color of lilacs with crystals that seemed to be growing. A labyrinth is especially helpful for lost wanderers or those of us experiencing withdrawal, confusion or anguish, for seekers walking the path of life looking for answers. For those of us who can't sit still in meditation with a gentle smile on their face breathing in and out.

To practice walking meditation through a labyrinth, you just put one foot in front of the other, over and over again, because that's all you know how to do anymore. You stay on the path. You eventually notice that you are, indeed breathing in and out. You eventually notice that you are, indeed, moving forward, and that surely, some amount of time has passed. The darkened void within shrinks or shifts slightly, but now you notice that the pain you feel might pull you to your knees. So, you just keep putting one foot in front of the other, over and over again, until you find that you can move in sync with your breath, and things begin to feel just a little bit better. As you move forward with your breath, you start to think that you might actually be going somewhere, as long as you stay on the path. And eventually, you reach the center of the labyrinth where you see a space or a stone bench and finally sit down to rest.

In front of you, there are piles of stones and crystals, offerings of coins, photographs, necklaces, and charms of various sizes and values. A statue of Buddha, sitting still in meditation with a gentle smile on his face, breathing in and out. Other people have been there too, before you, and decided to show their gratitude by leaving an offering. I took off my favorite sterling silver ring shaped like a horseshoe that ended in two circles, one small and one slightly larger, hanging out next to each other on my tan skin like a mother and child. "Thank you," I said, placing that ring on a special rock near the tranquil Buddha and stood up to find my way back out of the maze.

Pleasantly surprised that the path into the center of the labyrinth was the same path out, I then wandered meandering trails through the forest. Not knowing if I was missing a lecture or a class for my teacher training, dreading or perhaps wishing that maybe someone might wonder where I was, I stayed focused on my breakdown. For me, walking through woods seems to manage mental and emotional breakdowns better than pharmaceuticals can. I climbed an ancient oak to reach a simple but sturdy tree house. It was more like a platform with a railing, allowing you to stand safely and feel more capable of speaking directly to the Tree People, or just to yourself. The swaying peace of the treetops calmed me further. I needed to keep moving and found myself putting one foot in front of the other along another trail; past a pagoda, another shrine, a creek trickling over moss-covered stones. Finally, I found myself on a wooden dock, which turned at a right angle over a small pond. Again, an empty bench awaited me at the end, and I sunk into the splintered wood.

The pain became so unbearable that I felt a physical need to kneel, but I realized I was in sight of the glass wall of the lecture hall and people were milling about. Was I supposed to be mopping the kitchen floor or setting the table for the next meal? My head dropped into my hands where I could press my eyeballs deeply into my head and prayed. Nearby a shrine to Jesus, a small dirt path led to the other side of the pond I was facing. If anyone could heal this, why not you? Won't you help me? Can't you see how much pain I am in? Not only do I miss my daughter so terribly, but I have been trying to claw my way out of a loveless marriage for five years. I don't want to be here anymore. Please. Help. Me. Please help me. *Please*, help me.

The tears rushed like rain on a windshield, into my hands and down my arms until I could taste the salt. My heart was now at the bottom of the pond. A fountain floated out in the center of it, spraying a gentle but impressive mist that moved in the breeze. I stared at that mist for years, begging for him to retrieve my heart from the bottomless pond. I noticed that the air was still again, and the sun was shining. I felt warm and noticed a rainbow arcing out of the mist, held in the space over the pond. It was not a flickering rainbow, moving in and out of the mist or changing from any breeze. It was an image made for me to see in that very moment and held there, until I realized the truth. I was not alone. I was not wrong to want a truer, deeper Love in my life from my partner.

The truth was, I was already healed and had already found my way. The truth was that every step of the way, I am accompanied by this loving force and will be met, right where I am, when I call out for help. I was not lost. I was not broken. My heart was not a sunken treasure out of reach but busy healing wounds and growing stronger every day. Somehow, my heart had been seen. My voice had been heard, and my wounds had been tended to. The rainbow in the fountain gave all of this to me in the few moments it held its space there above the pond, somehow, showing me clearly all that I needed to know. The rainbow in the fountain shifted my path just a bit further, let me breathe again, and gave me what I needed to stop shaking and crying long enough to move forward, one step at a time.

Come Here, Go Away

"Your grief for what you've lost lifts a mirror up to where
you are bravely working. Expecting the worst, you look, and
instead, here's the joyful face you've been wanting to see.
Your hand opens and closes and opens and closes. If it were
always a fist or always stretched open, you would be para-
lyzed. Your deepest presence is in every small contracting
and expanding, the two as beautifully balanced and coordi-
nated as birdwings." — Jalal al-Din Muhammad Rumi

Lisa Broderick was a Brazilian-American, vegan chef
who studied with Sri Dharma Mittra, founder of the
Dharma Yoga Center in New York City. She was a certified
yoga teacher in her own right, but was the resident chef for
our yoga retreat. She was rather quiet and reserved, busy in
the kitchen the first few days of the retreat. She was smart
and thoughtful, not to mention a phenomenal chef. Many of
our meals were lovingly crafted from the fresh produce of
local farm stands and roadside markets when mid-summer
sweetened every growing thing. Fresh greens, donut peaches,
carrots, and tomatoes…it was like eating sunshine, fresh rain,
and cool breezes. Every bite was healing and wholesome. Lisa
poured a loving awareness into her cooking like some good
witch's healing potion. Before we ate a meal, we stood around
all the food laid out on a long table, thanked the chef, and
marveled at the freshness and color of the foods being of-

fered. A deep breath and a long, Sat-Nam, palms together at the heart, we blessed the food and the moment. This felt foreign and strange at first, but I relaxed into it, wanting to embrace new traditions and possibilities. This sacred sound, the food, the colors and the sun, the people, all contributed to the tincture that nurtured the healing of my heart.

But these wounds were still fresh, still very palpable—as though some metaphysical part of myself was broken. Even if you could grab hold of it, the pieces were splintered and infinite, all efforts futile. Who here could teach me how to pull all these pieces back together? Lisa shopped and cooked for us, kept the kitchen stocked, the tea ready, and she joined us on her mat in the back corner of the room for classes until, eventually, it was her turn to teach. Lisa taught us about the chakras.

The places along the very midline of our bodies where energy from the body-mind swirls into pools, forms color and vibration, can flow freely or be blocked, and is ever-changing. Each chakra correlates with psychological development, emotional and physical well-being, and will hum with a specific musical note. Sitting inside an open-air pagoda in the forest, we hummed strange sounds (Sanskrit "seed sounds") and focused on the rainbow of colors that traveled up our spines. I felt alive again for the first time in ten years. Humming with life, we were surrounded by a living forest that was humming right along with us.

Later, Lisa led us through additional activities so we could better experience our own chakras. Anahata, or the heart chakra, is a powerful place in the human body when healthy, and a destructive one when blocked or damaged. Lisa asked for someone who felt strong in their heart chakra. I was the only volunteer. Looking back, my ego must have raised that hand, or maybe I was blinded by my recent discoveries and insight, hungry for more healing, wanting those pieces to fly back together as quickly as possible. "Yes, do this, it will fix you!" whispered Ego.

She looked at me quizzically, "Are you sure?" I nodded and sat in front of her on the floor, cross-legged. The other students stood around us in a circle, watching intently, note-books and pens in hand. "Okay," she said, "hold my hands." We interlaced our fingers and pressed our palms together, sitting face to face, quite close, surrounded by fellow students. "All you have to do is repeat after me, but if you don't mean what you say, you won't be able to do it. Understand?"

"Um, I think so?" I nodded to reassure myself. What the hell did I get myself into here? "Repeat after me," she said, as she pushed her hands into mine, "Come here," and then she pulled our hands away from my chest, with a steady gaze into my eyes as she said, "Go away." Again, she repeated the simple phrase with each small, yet powerful gesture. "Come here," our hands pulled into my rib cage, chest, and heart, "Go away," as our interlaced fingers pushed away from my center and toward hers. "Now you," she said.

"Come here," I said, as I pulled in as if rowing…but the words got stuck somewhere below my throat—in my chest. My face contorted like a painful twist had entered my gut. I felt our small crowd step closer, a hand on my shoulder. My lower lip quaked and quivered as I fought to pull the words up, up, as I pushed with all my strength toward her and away from me like a deadlift. "Go, …away," I eked out as tears broke the surface and my head tipped back.

"Again," she said, looking into my eyes like a concerned friend, "You can do this." I bit my lip hard and nodded as the tears rolled down, dripping onto my forearms and thighs. "Come here," I pulled her toward me, took a deep breath, and mustered more strength to lift the heaviest phrase I'd ever uttered, "Go…Away," I repeated. With a few more reps, I realized how easy it was for me to love, to let others in, and how difficult it was for me to let them go, to say goodbye, or insist on their departure. Exhausted after just a few minutes, we released our hands, and I used my palms to shuttle the salty tears from my cheeks and neck. I felt hands gently rub my back.

"That was so amazing," someone said. "I'm so proud of you for doing that, thank you," said another. It felt like what an actual, supportive family ought to feel like. "You're so brave," said one of the older women, "I'm not sure I could have done that."

I shrugged my shoulders, smiled through the tears, and thanked them.

Findings

"What began it all was the bright bone of a dream I could hardly hold onto." — Michael Ondaatje

The summer before my senior year in college, I spent some time with my mom and was in her kitchen when my father called. This was a rare occasion, so I sat down by the window, noticing the sunlight streaming in.

"Do you want to see the bones of a mastodon?" he asked.

"Yeah, sure! Of course I do," I responded with excitement and curiosity because I wasn't exactly sure at that moment what a mastodon was.

"Good, well, come over and bring your camera," he instructed.

A gentle rain was busy making nature sounds on the roof of the barn when I arrived in Bloomfield that morning. The first odd thing I noticed was not a mastodon, or bones, but a real, live reporter. He was there to share the story unfolding at our feet. He was holding an umbrella in one hand and a microphone in the other. If I was correct, this was Doug Emblidge, the news reporter I'd seen thousands of times on our television screen at home, standing here in my father's barn.

When I looked down, I saw large, plastic tarps of blue and brown, laid out like a picnic beneath a spread of enormous, muddy bones. I began snapping photos as I listened to my father talk. "Can you believe it took four men to lift this part out of the mud?" he exclaimed, kneeling beside a skull the size of a small Volkswagen beetle.

I couldn't believe my eyes, but knew that all I had to do was shoot and listen, which was perfect. I'd been struggling to come up with a thesis for my senior art show and felt that this could be it, right here on the barn floor. If Doug Emblidge thought it was a decent story, then maybe my college professors would too. I quickly used up my only roll of film and we walked to the dig site where 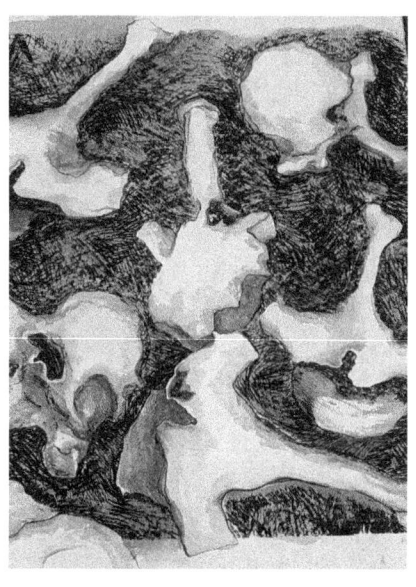 my dad and a hired hand had been busy excavating a pond.

When I was a young child and still lived on the farm, my parents still married, the family unit still intact, with our love-ly, lively pond; I felt alive. I can still recall it bursting with life, adorned in cattails and giant weeping willows, teeming with fish, and the odd turtle or two. I always hoped I'd get to see the Great Blue Heron, but that was infrequent. My dad would bring my brother and me down to the pond, climb into our white, wooden rowboat and float out to the middle. "Don't dangle your toes over the edge," he'd tease, "a snapping turtle might bite them right off!" I wasn't sure if there really were snappers down there, but I didn't want to sacrifice any toes to find out. Instead, we'd cast our fishing lines and pull in small rainbow trout, sunfish or small mouth bass. Freddy and I would lament how small our catch was and always set them free, into the darkened depths below, hoping they'd grow into fish the size of sea lions or dolphins.

One day, my dad told us he had a solution to the small fish dilemma and showed us how he'd set up a cistern in the old stone well in the dirt cellar of our ancient farmhouse. He placed a tube down into the water to pump in oxygen, a waterproof light so we could see the fish, and a few small trout. We were overjoyed just to be near these spectacular creatures, and every night we fed them fish food and noticed their growing bodies. Once they were too big for the small cistern, we'd return them to the pond hoping to catch them on our lines once again. This became our thing, fishing in this way with our dad.

After the divorce, ancient farmhouse fixed up and sold, my father remarried and put down new roots on forty-five acres in the village of Bloomfield. It had everything he wanted: fields for planting, some woods for tracking and hunting, but it was missing one key element: a pond. After raising trout in some large metal troughs in the basement and a run-down above-ground pool beside the barn, my dad hired an acquaintance with an excavator to dig a pond. A big pond, deep enough for fish to winter in its depths and grow large enough to be a prized catch on our lines.

This was a big project for my dad, and he had every detail worked out, until the unexpected happened. When they pulled out the first three-foot long rib bone, they thought it was a dinosaur. "Just my luck," my dad expressed his dismay, shaking his head. Instead of calling local scientists for advice or guidance, he dug those bones up himself, loaded them into his '59 Ford pick up and drove them over the hill to unload them in the barn. "They'd been in the mud for all those years, so I thought it'd be wise to keep them damp," he said as he pivoted side to side misting the picnic of bones with a hose.

As my father tells it, Paleontologist George McIntosh of the Rochester Museum & Science Center came out to see these bones and began to bang his head on the back of his muddy pick-up when he realized they were not in the ground anymore but  in his truck and strewn across the barn floor. Many of the skeletal remains were lost in the mud since they resembled stones, and my dad and his buddies missed many of them. Their hound dog, Chester, found one, though, and brought it home.

This part of the story was actually picked up by the *National Enquirer*. The article was titled: "No Bones About It, This Is Dog Heaven." "Chester the pooch is on top of the world as he sniffs a pile of huge mastodon bones found on his owners' farm. The Buchholz family unearthed the remains while digging a pond on their property in Bloomfield, N.Y. The yellow Labrador helped to uncover the bones—which belonged to a relative of modern elephants that lived about 8,000 years ago. The excavated bones were grouped together before being shipped to a museum."

Chester was actually a Redbone Coonhound mix with giant floppy ears and a heart of absolute gold. He used to catch fish in the great cave of his mouth he'd open under water, pick them up for a moment, and then carefully release them back into the pond. If you told Chester to drop something he had clenched in his teeth, he'd lay it gently at your feet, which is what he did with the mastodon toe bone. Mastodons may have been relatives of today's elephants but died off about eleven to twelve-thousand years ago due to climate change and over-hunting. The RMSC's carbon dating showed that the Bloomfield mastodon remains were roughly fifteen-thousand years old and belonged to a forty-five-year-old male who'd gotten stuck in the mud and fell quite easily to the prolific Paleo hunters of its time. Tool marks on the bones were signs its flesh had been used for food, its body kept in the cold water of the pond for refrigeration.

My father dug a pond in the exact spot where a pond had been fifteen thousand years ago. Where a frightened mastodon, left behind and stuck in thick mud, was attacked and killed, feeding an untold number of indigenous people. I think about who they were, what they wore, where they slept, and what wonders of nature they witnessed in their lifetimes. How were they led through life? How often did they move?

Did they have soulmates, partners, friends? Did they see Great Blue Herons way back then? Did they follow stars at night and lay on the grass watching our changing skies in awe as we do today?

I drove back into the city to my mom's house to tell her about the find and stayed awake thinking for many nights, writing and sketching. My thesis was given to me with a phone call from my father. A deep longing to know him was still alive in me and this felt like an invitation to forge something real between us. Or, at least, it was a way for me to make meaning of our relationship he'd buried long ago.

Hummingbird Spirit

"One can never consent to creep when one feels
an impulse to soar." — Helen Keller

An opportunity to participate in a Lakota sweat lodge ceremony was presented to us upon meeting the owner of the retreat center in Virginia. It must have been at least a week into our yoga teacher training at this time, and we were beginning to feel high on continuous yoga, deep breathing, and donut peaches. As she described how she became a certified Lakota Shaman, she asked how many of us might be interested in participating in the sweat lodge. She had been trained by Native American healers and certified through special rites so she could properly lead a sweat lodge, or Inipi, ceremony. Apparently, it was a very healing process I knew almost nothing about. I leapt at any adventurous possibility for healing, as did most of my cohort. We were instructed to fast the day of the ceremony, drink lots of water, and that we would build the sweat lodge as part of the ceremony. We would meditate beforehand and prepare ourselves for this sacred ceremony. I was intrigued and tingling with excitement at the possibility that I might leave this place with answers about my life.

Most of us elected to participate in the sweat lodge ceremony. We took our preparation instructions seriously and arrived with anticipation and hopeful hearts. It seemed we were all looking for answers. We came dressed in layers of loose clothing, as instructed. Water bottles in tow, unsure what to expect. I remember sitting down on a large blanket someone had laid out on the grass for us. Our Shaman guide had animal spirit cards for us to choose. She asked us to meditate on a question we had and to hold it in our hearts. "Where there is love, there are no questions," came to mind, but ultimately the questions I settled on were, *What do I do? Do I leave my husband? Do I ask for a divorce?* The card we chose would be our animal spirit guide through the healing journey of the sweat lodge ceremony. I held this and many questions in my heart like an overstuffed grocery bag stretched dangerously thin.

I chose a spirit animal card and flipped it over. It was the Hummingbird. A symbol of joy. This rattled and confused me. Joy? *Really?* I felt so very far from joy that I couldn't remember the last time I felt any. Moments with baby Ada in the bathtub as she played with the water flowing from the faucet, or my sweet dog Henry leaping for joy when I arrived home after a long day…these fleeting, vanishing moments. How would I know it, let alone be able to follow it if and when it came to lead me through this ceremony? The Hummingbird, so…tiny. It seemed like an impossibly delicate thing to hold onto or to follow.

As I studied the card more closely, I remembered seeing some hummingbirds zipping around the landscape earlier in the afternoon. I noticed that they liked the Echinacea but never stayed long. Then I remembered a moment I had inside the dorm room. I was alone in the bedroom full of bunk beds and exploded suitcases when I walked across the hall into the communal bathroom. I looked up and saw a hummingbird hovering just outside the small, square window. I froze to study it, to confirm that this was truly happening. A hummingbird hovering, facing me, as if it actually saw me, almost as if… it was choosing me. The next instant, it vanished. This sudden memory was like finding an elusive puzzle piece, as if some clearer picture was beginning to form, as if this spirit guide may be meant for me after all.

Our celestial-looking Medicine Woman taught us about the sacred ceremony of the Lakota people, or Inipi. The first Inipi was taught by the White Buffalo Calf Woman, who appeared to two Lakota as they waited, starving on a hillside. The White Buffalo Calf Woman brought ways of healing to her people, and what became sacred ways to reconnect with the Holy Spirit or Great Creator. The ceremony was described briefly, and she went on to explain how the Lakota revere the rocks and earth as beloved ancestors. The Rock People were there to keep us steady and strong, to keep us on the path of the spiritual journey, and would be gathered together with reverence and gratitude.

A circle of large gray and white speckled stones were arranged around a small pit that had been dug into the earth. The pit was then surrounded carefully by the Rock People, one at a time. A large fire was built and lit in the center. As we watched the fire die down and settle, we began to cover the willow-branched dome frame with layers of blankets. Traditionally, these would have been animal hides. Layer after layer we covered the dome with quilts and heavy wool until no light could be seen from within and we had constructed our sweat lodge. Rocks were added to the white coals of the fire and silently, we entered the lodge. Settling into a close circle around the warm glow of the fire, we each made our space around the outer edge of the lodge with little or no room between us.

The Grandfather rocks, white hot from the fire, were placed in each cardinal direction around the central pit inside the lodge. The fire outside the lodge dwindled as more white-hot stones were brought inside and placed in the center of the pit, one at a time using a long-handled shovel. Fresh herbs like sage and cedar were sprinkled onto the white-hot stones. A ladle full of water was gently poured over the stones, sizzling into purifying steam which quickly filled the dome. I wondered briefly how I would be able to breathe at all, in such dense steam, very little air coming in or out. The blanket door lowered, and our lodge transformed into a cave of darkness, bringing with it a sense of deep safety. No one could see anything or anyone, which, surprisingly, comforted me. We quickly relied on our sense of hearing, smell, and touch, leaving the world of sight behind. Our leader spoke with kindness, like a tour guide leading elderly tourists through a tough, uphill climb. She encouraged and pushed, left long pauses for us to consider an essential question with each round, and offered prayers and songs for every cardinal direction which reflected the indigenous teachings of the medicine wheel.

To the East: (The color yellow, representing spring and the element of wind.) Some who were nervous or scared sat closer to the door, knowing they could scoot out in between rounds without disrupting the ceremony if needed. I was squeezed between others in the center, across from and farthest from the doorway. Yet somehow, I felt quite at home. I would have happily dissolved in that steam if it meant I'd leave understanding my life better, what I needed to do next and how. Prayers were offered to the east, the season of spring and birth, sacred chants were sung, and we all took turns offering our prayers. Our voices seemed more powerful, more purposeful in the darkness. The prayers from our own hearts poured out like the water trickling over the hot stones piled up before us.

To the South: (The color red, the summer season and the earth element.) A lift of the door shocked us with light and cool air refreshing the space, marking the next round of the ceremony. Prayers of gratitude were offered to the South. More chants were sung softly, then more fervently. We again took turns offering our own prayers with the communal, "Aho," voicing our support and agreement.

To the West: (The color black, fall and the element of fire.) The darkness of the unknown, in which we had all become comfortable inside the lodge became more like a womb, or a place of care and connection. The four seasons are represented on the medicine wheel, as are the four stages of our lives. Fall represents our adulthood—the time we are independent, yet care for others, learning interdependence and deeper connection. Prayers and songs were offered with devotion and reverence once again, and we could sense our journey make an important turn through this round of the Inipi.

To the North: (The color white, winter, air, and the stage of death.) Indigenous cultures see life as a continuous circle, so the stage of death in our lives leads right into the next, or the springtime of birth or rebirth, so we were assured that this direction is a way to face our spiritual home—the spirits of the North bring one home to the Creator. With comfort, peace, and rest, at home we heal. Prayers and chanting were offered to the North, so sweetly, beautifully, like the sound of my daughter's voice. We again took turns offering our own prayers aloud, our voices merging into smoke and steam, offered up to the Spirits to guide us home after our journey was completed.

After each direction was acknowledged and revered fully, we were invited to open our hearts to our spirit guides, to sense them there with us. There was no colorful image of a hummingbird hovering high over my head like I'd imagined there would be. Yet, I felt just like how I felt earlier in the day, knowing that I was so close to a hummingbird that I froze. At this moment, I felt closer than I'd ever been to a physical hummingbird but did not see it. It seemed to be there by choice, ready to give me something. I thanked it for being there, and then I heard and felt the powerful rhythm of its wings, beating faster than I could ever count or move myself.

I began to feel this rhythmic vibration move down through my head and into my throat, releasing the hardened lumps of unspoken words. The hummingbird vibration continued down into my chest and hovered around my heart space where I felt a physical manifestation of pure, spontaneous joy. There are no real words to describe what I felt, but it was a physical vibration that was moving faster than a jackhammer and gentler than a feather, traveling down the center of my body, as if it was spreading joy outward. Joy was an emotion I was not sure I had ever truly felt before this. It awakened me to what I was missing in my life but what was also my birthright: The Joy of Being Alive. The joy of experiencing my daughter grow up. The joy of witnessing my own story unfold. The joy and beauty of the natural world offered to me every day. The joy of tasting fresh fruit or smelling the perfume of a flower. The joy of connection with the living earth and with others around me. My hummingbird guide showed me that Joy was there for me to access if I chose to, and now I knew what it felt like.

And then, it was gone. The rhythmic vibration of thousands of beating wings vanished as fast as a hummingbird darts to safety. Her job as my guide was done. With tremendous gratitude, I made another small pivot along my path knowing now that joy was possible. Enjoying life was indeed part of my future

Aces

"The wound is the place where the Light enters you."
— Rumi

"Trust in the power of heart and awareness to awaken through all circumstances." — His Holiness the Dalai Lama

Applying to work in daycare settings with young children made it necessary to document every place I'd lived for New York State to investigate whether any crimes or child abuse had occurred at those locations. Oddly enough, emotional abuse didn't count, just the physical, or else every address I listed would have set off alarms. *"Don't let this head-case work with kids!"* But no, any emotional or physical abuse I endured at the hands of my elder brother and mother was undocumented, my scars invisible to others. As an art teacher, I later learned about ACE scores, or Adverse Childhood Events, where any trauma is rated through a simple survey. Most people have at least a score of 1 on the ACE assessment, as traumatic events occur in all our lives. Only 15% of women, I learned, have a score of 4 or higher. I had a 4 and realized that everything I'd accomplished in life thus far was truly miraculous.

One trauma worth mentioning occurred while I was working at the Oregon-Leopold Daycare that was housed in a community center on Rochester's east side. I was fresh out of grad school, loving my independence and working with young children once again. I'd forgotten to bring anything for lunch that day and decided to go to the nearest corner store on my break. There was nothing I wanted to purchase, and I felt a weird vibe developing. I decided to leave without buying anything. As I moved toward the door I felt eyes on me. There were only men in the place, and I continued to feel a weight, or a sense of danger clinging to me as I walked across the street toward the community center. When I turned my head to look over my left shoulder, I didn't see anyone behind me. Yet, the feeling intensified. I turned my head to the right and saw no one but heard a man say, "Hey, gimme your purse." I turned my head to the left again and saw the business end of a gun inches from my face, held with a gangsta style elbow lift under a black hoodie. I was about to say, "I don't have a purse," but went silent when I turned my head again and saw the gun. I held up my hands and whispered, "take it," and the young man took my bag and fled.

Every life is a miracle. That young man was a baby once, a living miracle, all round and soft, utterly defenseless. His mom, too, and mine. My dad referred to my grandmother as a "yeller," meaning she yelled and screamed at my mom and everyone in the family. She had a deep need to control everyone and everything. It turns out, my great-grandmother killed herself at a young age. My mom never knew this happened until she found a newspaper article about it. For me, this explained why my grandmother was so strict and controlling all the time. She thought she was keeping everyone in line, safe and sound, like a drill sergeant, readying troops for battle. The only thing is, instead of feeling safer, you just felt scared all the time and tip-toed around the ultra-clean house, careful not to break anything, ever. My mom swore she would never be like her; that she would be easy-going and care-free, never yell or shout. A funny thing happens when you fixate on not being like someone: you focus on it so much that you miss what you do want to become. You leave yourself empty and vacant, trying desperately to keep what you don't want out, so that you become the very things you know best. Eventually, my mom also became a "yeller." She was never shown how to identify, express, or process feelings, or communicate her wants and needs, how to ask for help, or set boundaries. All of that was unheard of back then when she grew into adulthood in the 1960's. You kept your feelings to yourself. Or, more accurately, you denied your true feelings, pushed them down and bottled them up tightly, never noticing how they leaked out like acid, burning the ones you love most. Many American housewives of my mom's generation did not express or advocate for their own needs and wants in the realm of family. Many also denied they had needs at all. When you have no needs, no desires, no feelings about anything, it's a lot like you don't even exist—you don't feel seen, let alone appreciated. As far as Maslow's Hierarchy of Needs goes, it's unsustainable. I wonder what unmet needs this young man had when we met in the street that day, and how maybe, desperate enough, he thought he'd find what he needed inside a stranger's bag.

Leather deerskin gloves my father gave me were in that

bag. I never saw them again. My dad had his own issues. For one, he did whatever he liked, whenever it worked for him, and my mom was home alone with young kids most of the time. He had a freedom my mother did not. He played volleyball or basketball or lacrosse with friends after work while mom stayed home with the kids. She didn't get her night out or the chance to develop friendships of her own. Marriage and parenting wasn't exactly a team effort for them. Add piss poor communication, and adultery to the mix and, well, divorce was imminent.

One of my earliest memories is like a peaceful dream: golden-yellow leaves falling from the giant willow and maples in our backyard during a strong, autumn wind. It was pure magic to me, as a toddler, holding onto the windowsill to keep my balance, I can still remember it now. I also remember the sound of doors slamming, voices yelling, and the sound of distant crying. At a young age, I became sensitized to blissful beauty and the contrast of deep, emotional pain. From then on, until I left for college, hiding my endless stream of tears became routine, hardening into lumps in my throat.

The painful lump in my throat formed from things unsaid; Another way to discuss this psychosomatic response in yoga is through understanding the chakras, or energy centers in our bodies. I was experiencing a painful block in my throat chakra, and it had only worsened over the years. It came and went, but seared with pain most when I was in a romantic relationship with a man. This hot lump of pain in my throat existed for many reasons: my parents' divorce, the emotional and physical abuse I received from family members, and my inability to speak up and stand up for myself, telling them either to "come here, or go away" when I needed to. Eventually, I learned to be a rather good co-dependent. A co-dependent is powerless over relationships yet tries persistently to rescue, save, "fix," and control other people, at the cost of a healthy, honest relationship with boundaries and clear communication.

Melody Beattie helped me understand it best when she said, "Many codependents, at some time in their lives, were true victims—of someone's abuse, neglect, abandonment, alcoholism, or any number of situations that can victimize people. We were, at some time, truly helpless to protect ourselves or solve our problems. Something came our way, something we didn't ask for, and it hurt us terribly. That is sad, truly sad. But an even sadder fact is that many of us codependents began to see ourselves as victims. Our painful history repeats itself. As caretakers, we allow people to victimize us, and we participate in our victimization by perpetually rescuing people. Rescuing or caretaking is not an act of love."

At this point in my life I didn't know or understand what codependency was. I was just searching for the next step in life, because I was terrified of doing life. I was afraid to go to the daycare center for fear of seeing the young man who mugged me. I was also afraid of not seeing him and feeling him sneak up behind me again. I was afraid I would never see this young man again, never hear his story, understand what his unmet needs were, or how he'd been victimized by others. For months I experienced PTSD symptoms. One day, in the grocery store when a friendly man waiting in line said something to me about the weather, I nearly wet my pants from fear. He was standing in line behind me where I hadn't seen him, and there I was again, in the middle of the street, on my lunch break, ready to die. I noticed my body setting off multiple alarms. Maybe, I thought, it was time for a change. And like mother, like daughter, I decided to move.

My gram sent me some newspaper clippings for art teacher positions in the Southern Tier that piqued my interest. Was I abandoning my kids at the daycare? Was this my personal version of white flight? Am I too scared to live in the city on my own now? How could I leave these kids? Reluctantly, I started interviewing for jobs deep in the country. To my surprise, I was offered one that required me to move an hour and a half south of the city, into the heart of the Southern Tier. I found this journal entry describing that moment I decided to leave the city.

On Moving to Alfred
I listen to Los Lobos as I pack.
Again I am packing
things that I do not want.
The telephone is silent but not
    waiting.
What is it that I want?
Inside of this music I am bending my knees,
    banging my hips on walls,
stepping my heels into the floor and I feel
    that I am no longer here
already.

Inside this music,
Rochester
is an exotic place
    where no one knows me,
the mistakes I've made.
I am somewhere special,
Where I am special.
Especialmente.
Here is where I sing and dance and move
    without inhibition.
Adonde nadie sabe mi nombre.
This is where I have no belongings
    only myself and freedom.
Trees, everywhere.
I am going home again.
Always home, where home is always
new. Or it is not, and again,
I am lost.
While lost I have ideas about making art.
Art that other people can see and
talk about, and
    walk away from.
One of these ideas comes from inside the
rhythmic bells and clapping of this song.
I want to play one instrument at a time,
in whatever way I can,
just to make sound happen.
I want to make marks in quick
movements for a moment within the silence that follows,

within the breath of that sound.
I want to experience artistic freedom.
Only when I've done that can I
teach something to others about it.
Their Art,
my art.
I want the children to see their voices,
I want to see my own.

August 19th, 2001

Before I left Rochester, I went to one last yoga class at a nearby fitness center. It was a rigorous workout that night and I lay on the mat exhausted in savasana. As I consciously let the fear around my heart melt away to my hands, I experienced a sudden and clear vision. I imagined the young man who mugged me laying next to me on his own yoga mat. We held hands for a moment, and he said, "I'm sorry." It felt real and sincere. "I forgive you," I whispered. Without looking at me, he smiled.

My parents left the Southern Tier to find jobs, to build their careers and complete their education. They'd both attended Alfred State College before moving to Rochester in search of bigger and better things. I was leaving the city and returning to their childhood home in the country. After living in cities and suburbs for decades, I did not expect this change, and I embraced it as a new adventure. Another pivot was happening along this journey of life! For years people wondered why and how I'd been born in Rochester, attended Harvard, and ended up in the Southern Tier, or "The Dirty AC," as some refer to Allegany county, one of the poorest counties in New York State. People would ask me, "how did you end up here?" Today, my short answer is, "I'm here because I want to be here."

Soon after I settled into my new house in Alfred, my beloved grandmother died of lymphoma. She was done taking all the drugs, done with the endless treatments; she was tired and ready to die. She went to bed in her little home in Whitesville where she'd raised her five children and outlived two husbands. "How long does it take to die?" she'd ask with childlike curiosity when I'd visit her on the weekends. While she lay waiting, my family filled her home, cooking and pouring tea and coffee, playing cards, talking and looking through photographs. Then, 9-11 happened. Planes crashed into the World Trade Centers' north and south towers in New York City, the pentagon in Washington, D.C., and finally, passengers took over flight controls from the fourth plane so it would not crash into D.C. This plane crashed not far from here in northern Pennsylvania.

Our school, like schools all over the country, went into emergency lock-down mode. All doors and windows locked, shades drawn and all voices silenced. A veteran, fourth-grade teacher next door to my art room came over and asked, "Do you know what's happening right now?" I thought she was questioning whether I knew what I was doing as a new teacher and answered honestly, "No, I have no idea." She motioned for me to come into her classroom and watch the television placed high on an a/v cart turned to face the corner of the room like a naughty child. I saw a horror I'd never seen before that led to George Bush's War on Terror. Now, suddenly, we were all traumatized, all terrified, all confused and lost in our own homes. Everyone's ACE score went up one more point on that day. Again I stopped sleeping, thinking of those who were still alive, buried in the rubble of skyscrapers.

Chapel Street

"Hold fast to dreams. For if dreams die. Life is a broken-winged bird that cannot fly." — Langston Hughes

Since we'd moved so many times growing up, I'd lost track of how many moves and where, exactly. It never truly felt like home, just another place to sleep. My dream was to have a home of my own, not just a place to crash, but a place of refuge, to build memories, to connect with others, a place to stay. When I was living in Alfred, I lived next to a small church called the Gothic Chapel. It was a lovely building to see everyday that brought me a sense of security and peace. I also had a fat cat named Union, who came from the endless stream of foster cats my stepmother cared for. I named her after Union Square, where I lived in Somerville, just north of Boston. I loved that place, and I loved this cat.

When my lease in Alfred was up, I searched for a house nearby and happened to drive by a little white house for sale in Almond. The house was on Chapel Street near the corner of Union Street. This struck me as no coincidence, so I stopped to talk to the woman sitting on the porch. I pulled up in my beater truck that was wrapped in duct tape. It was a rough little Nissan truck, but I loved it. My gram loaned me two-thousand dollars to get a car when I moved to the Southern Tier, and this is what I got for it. The passenger side door didn't open, so I'd roll down the window for Chad to climb in that way. We named it Stella, because we loved to yell it like Marlon Brando in Streetcar Named Desire. I walked up the sidewalk to greet the woman on the porch and introduced myself. "Hi there," she said, "I'm Stella. Would you like to see the house?" We moved in two months later.

When I met Chad, I thought his name was Rafferty. In my defense, everyone called him Raff, or Rafferty, even his mother. At GJ's bar one night, a friend of his asked me, "What do you call him?" as she nodded toward my new boyfriend.

"Rafferty," I said, bewildered. "Why?" I tilted my head with a look of confusion.

"His name is *Chad*," she said plainly. I felt my face flush as I realized this was the third man named Chad I'd dated, with disastrous results, and I instantly knew this would be no different.

Chad could stay sober for nearly two months, if and only if he was truly committed to the cause. After that, he would disappear for days, drinking himself into black-outs and doing any and every drug that appeared before him. That was the Raff everyone knew and loved. In the small college town of Alfred, there were plenty of drugs to choose from. I never wanted any part of that, but I let Chad move into my little rented house with me, and although I was in no rush to move forward with the relationship, the good co-dependent in me wanted to rescue, save or fix this man any way I could.

After about a year of going through the pattern of sobriety, falling off the wagon, arguing about his whereabouts or if he should be drinking at all, I realized one important thing. We were having problems in our relationship, not because Chad was an alcoholic, although that was certainly a predicament, but because I was codependent. Perhaps it was both. Maybe he needed a docile, non-boat-rocking co-alcoholic who would pick him up off the floor and laugh about it in the morning. I realized that was not me. Yet, I was the common denominator in all the relationships I'd had in the past. I was the one who was going to have to find the courage to change. This addict/codependent dance was another echo of all my romantic relationships from the past that reached deeply into childhood memories of my parents' door-slamming arguments. Even though I realized this, I still didn't know how to change it. Like a dedicated co-dependent, I decided I'd show *him* how to change instead.

I spent many years going to Open AA meetings saying, "Hi, my name is Kristin, and I'm powerless over alcohol." I listened and read and learned about human psychology, sociology, spirituality, trauma, healing, and recovery. I felt deeply connected to total strangers who bravely shared their stories, trusting every detail would remain in the room after the hour was up. I drank bad coffee from Styrofoam cups and leaned against walls listening to other people tell their stories and share their revelations. Eventually, I got angry at the alcoholics enough to question myself. I was disgusted that the alcoholic just needed to stay away from substances when I was addicted to unhealthy relationships. The illness was inside of me—how could I stay away from *me*? "You can't heal a sick mind with a sick mind," as one of the many slogans goes. Or one of my dear friend Ray's favorites, "A sickie and a sickie does not make a wellie." With time, I realized I was not an alcoholic, but a co-dependent, someone who was perceived as bat-shit crazy by many alcoholics. "They're the ones who really need help," said a speaker at one Friday night meeting.

Chad and I struggled on and off for a year or more before I told him to move out. I knew it was coming, since he'd been sober for more than two months and St. Patrick's day was just around the corner. He'd decided to celebrate early and continued on for a few days after that, not coming home, not calling, not answering his phone. A friend of his told me he was passed out on the floor when I called around trying to reach him. I made up my mind to tell him the next morning. "I want you to have your things moved out before I get home from school today," I said, shaking. As expected, he flew into a rage, breaking things, punching walls, and screaming obscenities. I left quickly and ignored my phone as it buzzed all day long while I taught elementary kids in the art room.

When I worked up the courage to check my messages, they were all from Chad. The last one said he was going to end his life by hanging himself in our apartment, so I'd "come home to his dead body. Then I'd really be sorry." I called his mom, who was already there with him. She and her brother had raced there after one of his violent, ranting calls. Chad had a belt hooked firmly to the chin-up bar that hung over the stairs that led to the loft from the kitchen in my little house in Alfred. They'd arrived just in time.

After that, Chad did a "90 in 90," or ninety AA meetings in ninety days. The people in Alcoholics Anonymous slowly saved Chad's life. He started to see more clearly, speak more honestly, and connect with me once again slowly, and tenderly. He moved in with his mom for this time, sleeping on her couch. Gradually, he revealed the person inside who was vulnerable, yet hopeful, wounded, and healing; angry, but forgiving. What kind of person would I be if I didn't give him another chance when he was fighting so hard for a new way of life?

My two-year lease was up, and I didn't want to rent another apartment. I wanted a home. A home of my own at last, with a yard and a clothesline, a window in front of the kitchen sink to look out at the vegetable garden, to watch the yellow leaves fall in autumn. The house on Chapel Street was not far from Chad's mom in the tiny town of Almond, New York. It was everything I'd dreamed of, and a reason to stop moving, finally.

Chad enrolled in a college program for an associate's degree in Golf Management. Not at all a profession that got me excited, but it was a goal, a sober, long-term goal, so we all supported it. I lived in our new house in Almond while he attended school in South Carolina, living in a small apartment there for eighteen months. When he returned to New York we got engaged. It was a long, four-year engagement that ended in a marriage I knew would not last. I thought perhaps it should have been annulled the very next day, but that kind of conflict was way out of my league. I mean, I was better, more honest, stronger, but I was a long way from fully-recovered. I was a practicing codependent with a lot to learn.

We were married on my birthday, the twelfth of August, in

a sweltering summer of rainstorms. The eco-resort known as Pollywogg Holler offered a lively time in the forest we could afford. The owners, Bill and Barb, were like loving grandparents, but were often high, and double-booked their calendar to host two weddings on the same day. So, we had to move our wedding date one week earlier, which happened to fall on my birthday. Luckily, it was the only dry Saturday in that month, so it worked out nicely. All our friends and family were there, and it was one of the most beautiful, surreal days of my life. I remember a tangible sense of letting go, knowing that I had no idea how this would unfold.

My dad grew and harvested all the flowers for the wedding and brought them in coolers to keep them fresh. I can still see the deep orange and magenta colors of the zinnias, and the warm yellows and browns of the sunflowers. I plucked lily pads from the frog pond in Whitesville to float in glass bowls on all the outdoor tables we placed under the giant, white tent. I borrowed all the tables and chairs from a church, made handmade, recycled paper for our invitations, and dyed a blue streak in my hair for the "something blue" I needed for luck. My Aunt Sandy gave me an old pearl necklace to wear, and we sewed it into straps for my "something new" dress. This sounds crazy, but I think I was just as caught up in creating a fairy-tale wedding in the forest as rescuing this alcoholic from complete and total destruction. Or maybe I thought these two fantasies were one in the same.

Chad was supposed to make sure he did one thing: buy red ties for his three groomsmen. Chad's brother, Chris, his best-man, showed up late with a black eye and no tie. That was symbolic for me—or was it foreshadowing? Either way, I didn't like it. We enjoyed the day, praises and well-wishes from both our families, lots of pictures taken, and fell asleep without having sex. Or else, he fell asleep peacefully and I was awake, confused and distraught. Aren't you supposed to make love to your spouse on your wedding night? Aren't you supposed to be excited for that special connection as newlyweds?

I was beside myself with anger and resentment the next morning. Who takes care of every detail of her own wedding and is not cherished and made love to after the party's over? A good codependent, that's who. Annulling the marriage would be way too big a fight, one I was not capable of winning. But I considered it. Instead, I kept my head down and kept going to recovery meetings, reading the books, pleading in prayer, and changing ever so slowly. Maybe, just maybe if we had a baby, that would bring us closer together. My biological clock was ticking more loudly than ever, and even though Chad was not keen on having children, I convinced him that we should try. "If we get pregnant, it was meant to be, and if we don't, well then, it's not," I pleaded. We were pregnant by the next morning.

Ada was born through a traumatic, emergency cesarean section I was in no way prepared for. I wanted a natural birth—no drugs, just deep breaths and hand-holding. Our tiny baby had an unusually low Apgar score and was kept for two hours in the prenatal ward as I writhed about in the hospital bed, wringing my hands, unable to stand or walk from the epidural given that morning. For the next four years, my focus was on loving this child and pulling our family closer together. Yet, the more I tried, the more I found myself home alone with a colicky baby who had her days and nights reversed. Still, I loved her so, and I loved our home.

Our home in Almond was built in 1890 into the side of a hill on an old creek bed after the water had been diverted down another path to prevent the village from flooding. A giant, white Sycamore still stands proudly on Main Street and can be seen in black and white photos from over a century ago. Cool in the summer, and warm in the winter, the house was a refuge for wolf spiders and the occasional corn snake who inhabited the hill that is still, slowly swallowing the house. The master bedroom, however, was enormous. Our bedroom became my sanctuary. There was plenty of room to lay out my yoga mat and cushion and have a small altar to light a candle and incense. I created my own, private chapel on Chapel Street. I could look out one of the large bedroom windows into the side yard where I'd hung bird feeders and planted a small garden.

It was a dream of mine since childhood to have my own home, to have a place to stay and set down roots. Some people love moving their furniture around, redecorating and re-imagining the spaces in their home. I rarely did that, because I'd already done it so many times growing up: packing, un-packing, arranging, rearranging, it seemed refreshing just to leave it all the way it was, wake up the next morning and not have to pack up and move. It was my dream—to have a safe, warm home with a garden, a window in front of the kitchen sink, and family who'd visit and bring a dish to pass at Thanksgiving and Christmas. This was my dream, and I was holding onto it with everything I had.

Although Chad had quit drinking and doing drugs, he'd also quit going to meetings. He was *cured!* Pickled, as some old timers would say at meetings, "Once a pickle, always a pickle." Another childhood dream I refused to let go of was to be happy, and I wasn't. "I think I'm doing pretty great," he'd say, when I'd suggest a meeting. So, I went to Al-anon meetings on my own and later started a local CoDA meeting since there weren't any in the area. The more I focused on caring for and grounding myself and Ada, the greater the distance between Chad and I grew. We were two ships passing each other in the night, offering friendly greetings to and from. I learned how to do everything on my own. I could walk the dog and push the stroller simultaneously, get groceries, pay the bills, feed the family, and find time for myself. I began to realize that his absence was somewhat of a blessing. In a flash of anger one evening, he shouted at me when I attempted to hold him accountable for something. Face flushed and temper flaring, his rage was just below the surface, as he spat out words like weapons. Somehow, I stayed calm and steady, took a deep breath, and whispered, "And that is why I don't talk to you anymore." I left the kitchen shaking, but victorious. No more painful lump in my throat. I was learning to speak my truth. I realized that Chad wasn't the one changing anymore. I was.

When I tried to describe to Chad or Alysia or my therapist how I felt in our marriage, I told them that it was like wearing your favorite shoes for many years and you love them, but they hurt. It was like wearing shoes that were too tight or just didn't fit anymore. There were many nights after putting Ada to bed that I'd sit in prayer and meditation for hours on end. I painted a mural of the Virgin Mother Mary and added Om Shri Matre Namaha in gold over the curving background. I needed my mother to comfort me, but since that wasn't going to happen, why not her? How did she survive her grief? I learned to pray to her using the Hail Mary prayer so cherished by Catholics. I became close with the Holy Mother through yoga, however, and I began to recognize her as a universal mother—a loving mother to us all.

"Surround me with your loving arms…hold me in your heart. Let me know that I am loved, and that I can love. Show me that no matter where I go, I come and go in you. I am never out of your loving presence. That you are the smile behind the smile, the kiss behind the kiss. You are the constant presence that I forget until I remember, and when I remember my Self, I remember you…" Krishna Das was a constant source of grounding and redirection in my life, as well as the weekly yoga classes I was attending. The teacher, Cindi, became a close friend and encouraged me to practice as much as possible. My life became centered in yoga, prayer, and meditation. I called out to Mother Mary for help on the regular, and somehow, she was there for me. I could just feel her, from the heart of one mother, to another. I became stronger, more self-confident, and I was still devoted to making our

Om Shri Matre Namaha mural

marriage work.

When I wanted to talk about our marriage with Chad, it usually turned into a nasty fight that took days to recover from emotionally. He tossed pockets-full of coins into a bowl on his dresser, and one day I found a small slip of paper with the name Laura on it, along with a phone number. I put it back carefully, feeling like a spy. I asked him who she was. He denied knowing anything about it, called me crazy for the billionth time, and when I went to look for the paper again, it was gone. I was learning to let things go. I had learned to talk to my therapist, to journal, call my dearest friends and Alysia, go to meetings, use prayer and meditation, rather than tango with Chad's temper. I kept my distance, and I listened when the Dalai Lama said, "Trust in the power of heart and awareness to awaken through all circumstances." I remembered when one of my childhood friends told me, "We accept the love we think we deserve." I deserved real love in my life, not this one-way street. I began piecing it all together until I

Women's March Protest, January 21, 2017

was at long last ready for a separation.

I was terrified that he would fly into a rage. I was so afraid he'd wake Ada, asleep in her bed, and destroy her innocence. I had been sleeping on the couch for three nights after returning from the yoga retreat. It felt like I was sleeping with a stranger and I couldn't do it anymore. I finally decided to sleep in my own bed, that it was his turn to sleep on the couch, when I realized that he hadn't even noticed. When I explained that it was his turn on the couch, his rage emerged. I let it, warning him not to wake Ada. He refused to sleep on the couch in his own house, slammed as many doors as he could get his hands on, and screeched the tires as loudly as he could as he drove off to his mother's house. It was done. I had done it, or, at least, I had started the process and survived his rage.

We began marriage counseling and met at the office for an hour once a week to discuss our situation. He made small talk with the therapist, wanting her to like him. Chad needed everyone to think that he was a nice guy, or even, a great guy. He held his true feelings at a distance and never approached sincerity. He called me crazy in one of those meetings, and for the love of Mary, our therapist stood up for me. It's a rare occasion when someone steps up for you without being asked. "I think what Kristin is saying is that she feels needed by you, but not loved by you." Yes. *That was it!* How was she so able to sum up this complex web of feelings I felt so burdened with? "Yes," I agreed, "that's it." Chad looked at the clock and decided he needed to leave early. It was over, but I didn't know it yet. To me, our relationship seemed very much like a plant in need of water. Somewhere deep down, the roots were alive, we had a meaningful shared history, a blossoming daughter, but the whole thing was in desperate need of care.

Three months into marriage counseling, Chad wanted me to meet someone who might be helping him watch Ada on the weekends. He was nervous and stumbling over his words, and I got the feeling he wasn't telling me something. I paused and asked, "Are you trying to tell me that you've met someone?" "Yeah," he mumbled. "I've met someone. Her name is Laura."

This was the moment our marriage ended for me. It was akin to sitting close to a large gong sounding, the vibrations buzzing and waking every cell of your body. It was over. Ever so slowly I became grateful for Laura, because she was the reason I became willing to let it all go. I let our marriage, and the dream I had for our home and our lives together, go. "Let go and let God," as they say. And so, I did. It was the toughest thing I'd ever had to do, to let that dream go. To leave a marriage with a four-year-old child, just like my mom had done. What I knew deep down, though, was that my life didn't have to turn out like my mom's did. For the next two years I focused on my own recovery and caring for my precious daughter. With the help of Alysia, friends, my Yoga Teacher Training, counseling, meditation, and devotion to yoga and meditation, I began to heal. I did not just survive this time in my life, I learned how to love my life again, to feel joy again, and for the first time, I began to thrive.

Soon, there was a new narcissist in my life. Donald J. Trump. Allegany county in Western New York has always been a red county, staunchly Republican. Trump signs were as common here as bird feeders or rusty Ford trucks. After hearing how he spoke to Hillary Clinton during the presidential debate of 2016, I was shocked. Hearing how his supporters cursed women and paraded around with offensive signs appalled me. My mother, grandmother, and great grandmother would have all had some choice words for this man, as did I. My friend and I decided we would travel to Washington D.C. to join the first Women's March.

Two country girls navigating a big city was a bit daunting, but the waves of women and progressive supporters wearing pink "pussy" hats and carrying signs kept us moving in the right direction.

It had been many years since I felt so completely surrounded with sisterly love and support. I actually forgot such a force existed. When anyone stepped onto the train carrying a protest sign or wearing a pink hat, the entire train car cheered and applauded, welcoming them aboard. This adventure experiencing solidarity with other women changed me for the better. I felt a renewed sense of hope for the first time in a long time.

Patient or Prisoner

"Every year should teach you something valuable; whether you get the lesson is up to you. Every year brings you closer to expressing your whole and healed self."
— Oprah Winfrey

It was a Tuesday morning when my brother, Freddy, sent this text: *call me when you get a chance.* I called immediately, since he only texts twice a year on Christmas and maybe a birthday, if he remembers. "Mom fell last night and broke her hip," he said. "She is going in for surgery now." Here we go, I thought—this is the beginning of the end. I recently heard how mortality rates go up after a hip fracture. With Covid-19 still ravaging the country, no visitors were allowed in hospitals for any reason. This was the new waiting game, and one I'd rather not play.

Twenty-five days later, mom was still in the hospital recovering slowly. Calls and texts were a daily part of the effort to keep up-to-date on her progress or decline, and depending on the day, it could be either. Emails to the head nurse, Annette, often left us with more questions or frustration. Sometimes, when I called my mom's cell phone she would answer—usually if there happened to be a nurse in the room who could help her with such a confounding device. Sometimes, if we talked long enough, I realized she was somewhere else in her mind, not in the light blue hospital room with a lamp on the bedside table and calendar art framed on the walls. She was on a bus trip, and they were waiting to place their orders for dinner.

"Really?" I asked. "Who's with you on the trip, mom?" "Oh, let me see, it's all the ladies from my exercise class! I don't know who is in charge of dinner tonight, and I didn't bring any of my paperwork on it, so I don't know who to call. I should let you go so I can figure out who's in charge of dinner," she told me. "Okay, mom, I love you. Be careful and call a nurse before you go anywhere."

Annette put a special bracelet with a sensor in it on my mom's wrist, so if she got on the elevator it wouldn't move. Apparently, she's adventurous and makes the effort to escape not only from her room, but the entire third floor. She told Annette she needed to wait in the lobby for the colonel. After that she was awarded the special bracelet with a built-in sensor.

The last time I talked to her, she sounded positive. She was a little upset about her discharge date being moved again. This time, she had a slight fever. Now she is on antibiotics and doing better, so maybe next week. Now it's next week again. Another text, she's fallen again. It's starting to feel more like a prison sentence than a hospital stay.

A social activist group called MomsRising asked via email, "How has the pandemic affected you or your family?" This is what I shared: My seventy-seven year-old mom's health had already been declining before the pandemic hit in March of 2020, but now, a year later, I have only seen her once very briefly. She has aged a decade in one year. Her Parkinson's is winning battle after battle every time she falls or forgets simple things. All of her exercise classes were canceled, therapists and teachers were limited and her sedentary, winter lifestyle of reading and baking set in. She fell and broke a hip in January and was rushed to a local hospital for surgery. After a partial hip replacement, she was expected to return home within days. Unfortunately, months later she is languishing away in a long-term care unit in the hospital, unable to stand, walk, get around independently, or return home. Physical therapists and nurses are caring for her the best they can, but they focus on her hip, her mobility, and not the Parkinson's disease. We have never once spoken to a doctor or neurologist. Countless emails and phone calls have been made by me and other family members, often ending in greater confusion, frustration, and helplessness. Tonight, I feel helpless. A recent conference call informed us that due to a slight fever, she could not receive her second Covid-19 vaccine shot. This pushed her discharge date back another week. A recent text informed us that she had fallen once again, washing her hands from the wheelchair in the bathroom. No cuts or bruises this time, though. She has fallen half a dozen times since she's been in the hospital, yet we are still unable to bring her home. When we can, I would like to be there to care for her as much as possible. All I want is to see my mom again and care for her while she can still recognize me as her daughter. Please help us. Thank you.

Writing and sharing what my mom was going through was cathartic, but it didn't change anything right away. By this time, I was fully vaccinated and waiting for the chance to volunteer in the hospital just to see my mom again. It seemed like she was never going to be released and might die in there, whether it would be Covid-19 or Parkinson's that killed her was unclear. Eventually, my mom fell so frequently in the hospital setting it became obvious they couldn't help her anymore and released her to my stepdad, Evan. She did much better and worked hard at her physical therapy once she was home.

A remarkable Physical Therapist named Sarah helped my mom get stronger and more able to maneuver herself around the house. Eventually her walking improved so she could leave the wheelchair behind and hobble around "counter-surfing" and occasionally using a walker. The hallucinations continued and managing her frequent medicine doses was difficult. We set alarms on their iPad to go off when she was supposed to take the medicine and my stepsister, Grace, a pharmacist, set up all her medicine in daily pill boxes so they were organized and ready to go. Unfortunately, if you don't know what day it is or have any sense of time, taking medications five times a day becomes nearly impossible.

When my mom misses the carbi-dopa or leva-dopa that masks her Parkinson's symptoms, she talks about where they're hiding human remains or how they're turning the farm into a giant speedway. Evan pulled out some old turkey decoys he used for hunting and propped them up in the flower gardens around the farmhouse. My mom would look at one of the turkeys and talk to it like it was a real, live bird. She would even hear it make gobbling sounds like a real turkey and remark on how noisy it was. Once, she said she saw a pig out on the porch. I went to look, just to be sure, and told her there was no pig on the porch, no boy out at the mailbox, no old man sitting out in their car. Sometimes, she just needs to investigate and see for herself, so she hobbles out of the house to go talk to the ghost-boy at the mailbox or see the 1950s Ford truck parked in front of the barn for herself. Thank goodness, at this point, she does not have car keys or the ability to drive. What was once a tragedy is now a blessing.

One afternoon, my mom ventured out to talk to the young boy she sees lingering by the mailbox. She sees this young boy by the mailbox regularly, but no one else has ever seen him. Somehow, she made it down the gravel driveway without falling, across the busy, two-lane highway without getting hit by a car or speeding truck to reach the mailbox, only to tumble into the deep ditch along the roadside. A perfect stranger driving by saw her fall and turned around to help. "She was strong, that woman, she pulled me right up outta that ditch," mom marveled. No harm done this time, but she could have been killed. Adventures like this get the whole family talking, group texts buzzing phones late into the night. "How can we get them more help?" "Who can go out for a visit?" "Did she need to see a doctor to make sure nothing was broken?" "What did Evan say?" "Where was Evan, anyway?"

She's not supposed to be left alone, we'd remind him, and his response eventually became, "There's someone here on the farm 24-7, she's never alone." Weeks later, my mom tumbled head over heels down their concrete steps that lead from the kitchen out to the circular drive between the long, red barn and County Route 41. This time, Evan was there. He picked her up, brushed her off and said, "She looks fine to me!"

We have all been taking turns going to the dusty old farmhouse that smells like cow manure outside and cat urine inside; cleaning, cooking, shopping, preparing meals, checking piles of mail, and helping to pay bills, do laundry and find things like keys, cats, catalogs, phone numbers, cell phones, credit cards, and pill bottles. Oh, and the cats…*six* cats. Two of which hid from all humans except my mom. Since my brother and I were the only ones cleaning litter boxes regularly but too infrequently, the cats shit along the outer edge of the large living room in the back of the house.

Radioactive Cats by Sandy Skoglund, 1980,
St. Louis Art Museum

Instead of picking up the mess or emptying litter boxes, Evan sprinkled baking soda on the piles of cat shit to "dry them out," and just left them there, glued to the shag carpet. There was always a new perplexing horror show like this to sort out. Eventually, I used Central New York's SNAP (Spay-Neuter Assistance Program) to take two of the cats whose names she couldn't remember and two others were escorted to the barn. This agreement took weeks and Evan swore and grumbled about the "damn cats" without helping until we came to this compromise.

Meanwhile, my mom developed an intense paranoia about her medications and believed someone was stealing them. For many weeks she hid the pill boxes Grace so carefully managed because she didn't want them stolen. Often, no one could find them when she needed to take her medicine. The third time she did this, when Grace had to replace the entire black, leather case that held a week's worth of medicine, I realized it was time for her to move to a safer place where she would get better, more consistent care.

Talking to my mom and Evan about receiving help was like walking on eggshells, you had to tread very lightly. They didn't *want* help, they insisted. The pandemic was raging on, so they didn't want strangers in the house, especially if they weren't vaccinated. They insisted that they didn't need the help anyway. Delicate negotiations often ended in compromise and an insistence on some level of help; whether it was two or three days a week for an aide to stop by and cook, clean, help my mom out of a chair and make sure she did her exercises… This, leaving the farm and moving out altogether, was a whole new proposition.

Luckily, I remembered an important part of my own story, which was prayer and meditation. Wishing from my heart for them to get the help and care they needed, over and over again, like one foot in front of the other through a labyrinth. Sitting with a stone statue of Buddha my dear friend Ray gave me, helps me clarify what's in my heart so there is a clear path ahead. Eventually, I was certain that moving my mom off the farm was the right thing to do.

I utilized a free service called "A Place for Mom" online and regretted it soon after. Emails and phone calls from directors of assisted living facilities started pouring in. Many residents in these facilities died from Covid-19 over the past year and enrollments dropped dramatically. They're desperate to get more residents and use liaisons to connect with families in need. It was a lot to manage along with my full-time job teaching art and being a mom. After the third major disappearance of mom's medicine, however, I decided she needed more care than any of these places could offer and told them all that I didn't want any of their help. I was thinking worst-case-scenario: she needs a nursing home and we're terrible people for waiting this long to make any moves to improve her situation. A persistent director by the name of Emma continued to email me, not with offers and deals, but with compassion and care. "Give us a chance," she said. So I did, and with any luck, we will be moving my mom into her new home in November.

Elderwood Village in Fairport is an assisted living center where a nurse is available 24-7, a geriatric doctor literally makes house calls, all meals are provided, laundry service and cleaning are available, exercise classes and group activities are free, and my mom, along with many other moms and dads, grandmas and grandpas, are never alone for very long. This was the place for mom. This was the opposite of what she was acclimated to: alone in her chair, unable to get up easily, struggling to dress herself, stumbling, falling and no one coming to check on her for hours, forgetting how to put a meal together or where her phone is, what medicine she'd taken or where she hid them. After quite a few talks about how good this would be for her, and that she should just give it a try for a month, she still did not agree.

That same week she was scheduled to get a booster shot for the Covid-19 vaccine. Grace reminded them the day before, and I had my mom write it on the calendar, where to go (her doctor's office) and what it was for. Evan drove her that day (Sunday, instead of Monday) to the doctor's office for said booster shot, and they were both baffled as to why no one was there. They were both utterly perplexed by dates and times. Because of this, I decided to wait to tell her the plan.

The plan was, whether she was willing to go or not, my brother Freddy and I were showing up, packing her things, and taking her to Elderwood for one month. We would convince her to try it for a month. Emma, the director, was familiar with this plan, gave us her full support, and all my prayers were channeled into "getting her out of hell" and into Elderwood. My plan also included calling her the night before we were going to show up so she would understand that there would just be one sleep before she saw us and took her to Elderwood to try it out. Two days before our move date, mom called and said she was indeed ready to go. She wanted to leave the farm. When I asked her what prompted this decision, she said, "Evan can talk a good game about being a good person, but some days, when it comes down to it, he can't even be decent." I wasn't sure what had happened, but our plan was set in motion with my mom on board. She was packed and ready to go when I arrived on Friday night.

Evan was confused about the whole thing. All he knew was that Pat was moving out. "This goes, and that goes, and both those cats. There will never be another cat in this house," he grumbled as he pointed to my mom's few pieces of antique furniture. Evan thought they were breaking up and we were moving her out. He simply would not accept the truth we continued to tell him, that she needed more care.

"The only thing we're bringing is her chair," I said, pointing to the gray recliner I bought her for Christmas. I had to explain it three different ways before he understood, but didn't like it. Grace came and got her dad out into the field to pick squash for a while so I could load up the car and get things moved out. We had a brief rendezvous in the driveway, filled with repressed emotion, eyes filled to the brim with tears, gave a round of hugs and we were off.

The GPS brought us north along a scenic route through pouring rain. After a night of approximately two-hours of sleep, I was still praying we could pull this off. "Please get us there safely. Please make this work out for the best. Please keep me alert and awake, please…" My prayers were answered, and my mom was settled into her new home in Elderwood that afternoon. I could barely believe it. I was invited to stay for dinner in the dining hall and cried through most of the meal as some residents chatted with us. "I'm just so relieved she's here," is all I could say. From now on, no one will be yelling at my mom on a regular basis. Her medicine will be given at the correct time, and she will be able to leave her room to find people pushing walkers around just like she is. She can sit down to play bingo or watch a movie with a group of her peers, get to know people in the dining room or stay in her room if she wants. For me, all this meant tremendous relief after two years of worry, drama, tears, missing medicine, too many arguments, and far too many falls. When I asked her how she liked it so far, she lamented, "I miss my cats."

One day later, I was back to teaching full-time, being a mom, walking our pandemic rescue dog named Thor, teaching yoga, and getting through with a lot less stress and worry, until my students decided that instead of yoga, they all wanted to knit for the class period. "Sounds great to me," I said as we sat on the floor laughing and learning to knit hats together. The trial of Kyle Rittenhouse came into the conversation, and I soon realized that I had very little understanding of the trial and what had actually happened that night in Kenosha, Wisconsin. I also learned that my students thought he, a young man of seventeen who killed two men and seriously injured another with his AR-15 rifle, was a *hero*. This understanding, that my students and I existed on opposite sides of a great chasm, broke me. When I say it "broke me," I mean, I once again became an insomniac.

When I struggle with insomnia, anything I do to bring upon sleep simply fails. Taking sleep medication, listening to soothing music, sipping bedtime teas, alcohol, journaling, yoga, meditation, all fail. My mind is not racing, it is stuck in a state of absolute dread and misery believing that everything I'm doing in my life is meaningless and futile. The story of "I've taught my students absolutely nothing, so what is the point of my entire life anyway," is not just a story but an indisputable fact I need to stay awake to digest slowly and painfully. *I suck. The world sucks more than I ever thought. My life is a waste…*

At about three a.m. I called in for a substitute to teach my classes the next day, and at about five a.m., I emailed lesson plans to the appropriate parties. For almost two years now, teachers have had each other's backs constantly, in a world that is dangerous and unpredictable. Perpetual quarantines, unimaginable sickness, deaths, and ongoing trauma from this pandemic has taken its toll. I texted my art teacher friend, Rhiannon, my next-door neighbor, my "roommate," as we called each other, and told her that I was broken. "Whatever you need. Take care of you today," was her response. Every opportunity I could, I chose to step up for her and say, "I've got you, don't worry." That support came back to me in that moment. That little hit of unquestionable love and support was enough to put me to sleep for a few hours, and slowly, over the next few days, I recovered from being broken. I have a great therapist to whom I am so grateful, but it was Alysia who broke down this break-down and pushed me further along this most recent path of healing.

"I know this isn't the same thing, but it reminds me of when Kevin was sick and he was going through that intense treatment and was so tired all the time. He just worked and came home and slept. It was all he could do to get through the day. Taking care of the kids, cooking, cleaning, shopping, everything was all on me. I did it for a year, and I was just white knuckling it for so long that once I realized he was getting better, I was able to really rest. I let my guard down finally and allowed myself to relax. Soon after that I was an emotional mess. I just fell apart. I realized later it was because I had been holding everything together by myself for so long, experiencing this chronic stress and worry for so long that I didn't allow myself to feel, to grieve, to ask for what I needed or wanted…I just kept going. Once it was all over, I felt it all. All the emotions, all the worries and fears I kept pushed down because I had to. I think this is what's happening with you now that you know your mom is somewhere safe."

I took a deep breath and told her I thought she was spot on. I was recovering from the chronic stress of many layers of uncertainty: the global pandemic, moving, supporting my mom from a distance, and finally getting her moved into an assisted living center where she would be safer and cared for. I had finally reached a place of deep letting go, which was much like sitting at the center of the labyrinth, knowing that you can rest there for as long as you want, but that you'll have to get up and keep moving eventually. With deep rest and relaxation, gratitude blossoms. Gratitude gives rise to a humble amount of contentment. With this contentment comes hope.

With my mom tucked safely into a supportive community like Elderwood, nursing techs bringing her medicine at the right time, meals served daily, I could breathe again. And so, I began to fall apart. This realization helped initiate the process of healing. After a few days of practicing lots of self-care as if I were deathly ill, I began to feel stronger and more like myself once again. Yoga practice, meditation, some writing, a few really good meals, and I was me again.

Then, as if on cue, Covid-19 showed its nasty face again, this time at Elderwood. My mom was quarantined in her tiny room for fourteen days, without visitors. I called as often as I could, and she seemed okay with all of it. Once she told me she had been on a plane trip to New Zealand with all the grandkids. "Ada wasn't there, though, I think she was with her dad or something," she recalled. At least her hallucinations were helping her get through what might otherwise feel like a prison sentence with solitary confinement.

In reflecting on my mom's state of health and fragility, I prepare for the last years of her life, of *our lives*, intertwined. I do what the Stoics do, they imagine and feel all the emotions they may one day experience, as preparation, to steel themselves against the cruelty of life. I imagine what I will share at her memorial service. Maybe it will be something like this:

A few things I learned from my mom…

It is because of my mother, Pat Buchholz, that I am here today, that I enjoy a happy, healthy life, filled with love and gratitude. She showed me the importance of gratitude, kindness, perseverance, and how fleeting happiness can be unless it comes from within. There are some essential life lessons I learned from my mom:

The first is gratitude:

One of my mother's favorite phrases was "don't look a gift horse in the mouth." She explained that usually, if someone gives you a horse, you can bet it's not a young stallion but more likely to be a rather old, run-down, tired out horse who wants nothing more than to be left alone in the pasture. To find out for sure, you'd have to inspect this old horse's teeth and that would be rude. I mean, you're being given a horse, so you should be thankful, no matter what its age, whether it can give you a ride somewhere or not.

"Don't look a gift horse in the mouth" was uttered when we enthusiastically opened Christmas gifts to find new underwear instead of toys, were given hand-me-down bikes or clothing, or other less desirable, worn-out gifts. Any investigative questions about said gift always seemed to prompt, "don't look a gift horse in the mouth." And instantly, I pictured starving children, homeless veterans, and orphans. It worked every single time. It turns out that even the Dalai Lama teaches that practicing gratitude for what you have in life is one of the keys to happiness. Be thankful for what you're given, even if it is underwear or an old horse.

The Importance of Service:

My mom loved to drive fast. As I clung to the nearest handle, she liked to remind me that she missed her calling as a race car driver. But really, deeper down, my mom wanted to be a teacher, but her parents only had enough money to send one of their three daughters to college and it wasn't my mom. Yet somehow, my mom eventually did attend classes at Alfred State College, relying on student loans where she earned an associate degree in business and met my father on a blind date. As a single mom, she later completed her bachelor's degree in business at RIT. She worked hard to do her very best in all her classes and worked as a secretary at Eastman Kodak, a customer service representative for Xerox, and finally a legal secretary and full-time working mom in the 1980s and 1990s. My mom worked hard in stockings and high heels, and she rarely missed work despite severe carpal tunnel and endless migraines.

She scrimped and saved so she could take me and my brother Freddy along with a friend of our choosing to Myrtle Beach every spring. It was always a total blast full of anticipation, excitement and of course, that long stretch of beach and beautiful weather. Mom would book the same hotel, drive pretty much the same route, and succeed in fulfilling her wish to treat us kids to a decent vacation ev-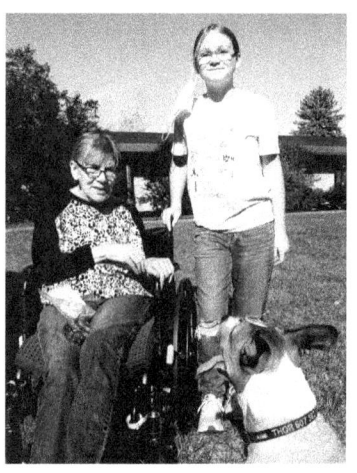ery spring. She did what she could, on her own, to give us that experience. My mother's sacrifice showed me more about gratitude than any physical gift ever could. My mom lived her life in service to us, her kids. We were what was most important to her, and we knew it.

The Importance of Kindness:

My mom suffered from a great many things. As I mentioned before, perpetual speeding, migraines and carpal tunnel, but also depression, anxiety, stress, guilt, shame, poor body image, high-heels and stockings, and later Parkinson's and dementia just to name a few. Yet, no matter how awful her day was, she would always hold a door for a stranger, say hello or offer a few kind words, be ready to chat with a neighbor, grocery store clerk or co-worker, or even invite them to Thanksgiving dinner. My mom held a deep compassion for the suffering of others.

When her friend and co-worker, Azid, did not have plans for Thanksgiving, she invited him to our small home in Rochester to share in the holiday. When she worked for Woods Oviatt Law offices as a legal secretary, my mom mentored a young man by the name of Juaquin. She took him bowling or out for ice cream, asked him about his life and was there for him as much as she could be as a mentor. I think she realized she may have gotten more out of the relationship than he did and was grateful for their companionship. Despite lifelong hardships, my mom continually embraced respect and kindness for everyone, regardless of age, race, or sexual orientation.

Generosity:

My mom was an incredibly generous person. She earned a decent salary but was given very little. She worked hard for everything she had and valued it. She was always willing to work overtime, take out a loan, or find a way to get us kids whatever we needed. When we needed new sneakers, she'd shriek and gasp at the price tags, but they'd come home on our feet. New boots and winter coats were imperative every fall, as well as back-to-school shopping. Somehow, she always found a way to check everything off her list.

My mom always encouraged me in the arts, complimenting every drawing I made. I have fond memories of laying on the floor coloring with her, talking quietly. She made it clear that I was to attend college immediately after high school and not make the same mistakes she did. With her help, I received student loans, grants, and scholarships that made it possible for me to attend Syracuse University and achieve a bachelor's degree in fine arts. When I was presented with the opportunity to study abroad, I asked hopefully, knowing that it would cost even more than the standard sky-high tuition, room, and board. My mom said that if it was something I really wanted to do, she'd get a second job and do whatever it took to make it happen, which is why I stayed in Syracuse. I hated asking for money, because I knew she would give it to me, even if she didn't have it. "Where there's a will, there's a way," she'd say.

One of her all-time favorite things to do was to choose an angel off the angel tree in Perinton Square Plaza at Christmastime and shop for them. She'd tell me again and again what was written on the back of the paper angel ornament: what the child's name was, how old they were, and what holiday wishes they had. She loved knowing that she could ease a young child's pain through simple acts of generosity. My mother knew firsthand that you get what you give, and it's because of this that I learned the importance of generosity—thinking more about what you can do for others, how you can help, and what you can do to uplift someone else, regardless of your own circumstances.

Happiness is an inside job:

Finally, I cannot say that my mom was never happy. There were definitely moments of happiness. When she got to travel with friends or family, seeing new places, experiencing new things, she was thrilled. She loved discovering new things about the world. When she held my daughter for the first time, rocking her on our front porch, I could see that she was genuinely happy. And I imagine she felt that same way when she held her other grandchildren, as well as me and my brother when we were babies, too. Most of the time, though, my mom searched for happiness in others–in her marriages, especially, or in her children, in her church community, in her dog, but very rarely in herself. Two divorces and never forgiving herself for mistakes she made created lifelong heartache for my mom.

Yet, she knew this wasn't quite right either, that at some point, you've got to move on, and she'd say to me, "Kristin, you can't wait for someone to give you roses. You have to plant your own rose garden." And I could see how much sense this made. You'd have plenty of roses for the bees, for your old horse to eat, and maybe a few for the dinner table too. My mom had the power to do things for herself, as we all do, but she needed a mirror in which to see her truth. I hope that my brother and I, as well as her grandkids, were her mirrors.

She preferred hydrangeas, by the way, and she had plenty, and her own backyard, a dog, and a quiet life she liked. Yet, living alone, she never seemed truly content. My mom survived tremendous loss and heartache, found ways to take care of her kids on her own, and that was good enough in my eyes. What I could see plainly was that the source of our happiness must come from within, from gratitude for what we have and for the love we experience in our lives, not from someone or something outside of us that's constantly changing. As John Kabat-Zinn put it, "all the suffering, stress, and addiction comes from not realizing you already are who you are looking for."

Soon after my mom's quarantine was lifted, my brother Freddy and his wife Emma went to pick her up for a Christmas eve gathering. They noticed immediately she'd been through it. The arm of her upholstered chair was torn, all the stuffing pulled out, photos removed from frames and scattered everywhere, her balance and mobility shaky and unreliable. Emma styled her hair and helped her dress. As they prepared to leave for Freddy's house, my mom slid slowly down the side of the bed, unable to catch herself or to get up off the floor without help. Emma helped her, and they continued on to the family gathering. My mom was surrounded by family, just as she wanted. Emma's parents, Don and Barb, her sister, and their family were there, and Freddy's three kids, Ryan, Holly, and Jack.

After returning to Elderwood, she continued her life as best she could, struggling to stand and transfer, to move in ways that could get her around slowly but safely. The Elderwood staff helped when they could. One morning, my mom fell in the bathroom and when staff came to give her medicine, she was unable to get up on her own. Their

Ganesha, Stained Glass Window by Cindi Kelly, 2013

policy stated that if a resident could not get up on their own, they must call an ambulance. On December 31st, my mom was admitted to Highland Hospital, a bit dehydrated, confused, feathers ruffled, but no serious injuries. I visited her bedside, in the hallway of the overcrowded hospital, trying to explain. She wanted to get up and go for a walk. The nurses said, "No, Pat, that's not safe." I helped her grab a railing and pull herself up just to stretch her legs. She did a few reps from standing to sitting on the edge of the bed. She needed to feel her feet on the ground, to stretch her long legs, to feel alive again.

The next day, we were told that she had been exposed to Covid-19 and placed in quarantine for eighteen days. When I visited her after the quarantine was lifted, she could no longer stand by herself, let alone go for a walk like she wanted to. The anger I felt at the hospital was like hot coals melting snow, like freezer burn. The frustration I felt became its own monster. Knowing that these healthcare workers, doing everything they could to help her, were making her Parkinson's worse every day by leaving her in that hospital bed; this became an aggravation I had to adjust and breathe through every day. They are doing their best, and they are making her worse. She cannot leave, she is trapped there, no longer a patient, but a prisoner.

I visited my mom at Highland Hospital whenever I could, bringing her flowers and snacks, and children's books to read to the imaginary kids in her imaginary play. She told me during one visit that she was worried about accepting the award for her screenwriting since it was being held so late at night. "Ten o'clock at night, can you believe that?" I didn't question her fantastic stories unless it was to show interest and tease out a few more details. I hung clothes up for her to see and reminded her to call a nurse before she tried to get up and go anywhere. Meanwhile, in the rest of the world, Covid-19 had killed over 900,000 people in the United States alone. The National Cathedral in Washington, D.C. was ringing a bell for every thousand people killed by this novel coronavirus. It took ninety minutes of nonstop bell ringing to represent that many lives taken.

And yet, many people I know, including my brother, believe it's all a hoax. "These people died of the flu or pneumonia or sepsis, something other than Covid-19. It's all a ploy to give millions of dollars to Big Pharma companies, research labs, and powerful corporations for vaccines and medical equipment, to make the rich get richer." Who knows, maybe he's right, but I don't think that many people can actually communicate and work together long enough to create a global hoax of any kind. I don't trust our government or anyone else's because they are never made up of the people, they are so often the wealthiest, most privileged, most entitled representatives money can buy, waving flags and covering up crimes to keep themselves and their friends out of trouble. Sometimes it seems like the whole world has dementia. I do, however, believe the doctor who looked me in the eye and said, "the best defense is to wash your hands, wear masks, and get vaccinated." And I believe the nurse, who gave me her cell phone number because she wanted to know how my mom was doing. I believe science when it has good research and consistent efficacy. We were all still scared to death at this point, having been to funerals and memorial services, after hearing about friends and family of co-workers in the hospital and not making it out alive. But we're tired. *I'm tired.* It's exhausting never knowing what to believe or what you can rely on.

Teaching is tough, active work, especially in the art room. My yoga classes offer a little respite, and I savor it, taking everything slowly. But the nine-period day with three precious minutes in between classes seems like a schedule for someone on Ritalin. I need to *chill.* I need to *breathe.* My nerves are shot with all my mom's crises and constant needs. My phone rings constantly about hospital updates, Medicaid applications, and power of attorney responsibilities. Teaching, balancing my mom's care, trying to be a decent parent and partner, takes everything I have out of me, every day. But I'm doing my best. We are getting through it. We survived Covid-19 without long-term symptoms. I sit on my closet floor in front of my concrete Buddha, and he calms me. He reminds me to breathe. He reminds me to be grateful—to want what you have, to savor these small, peaceful moments. Watching Ada grow up. Feeling loved by Dan. Having a partner I can lean on. Having true love in my life. I breathe in deeply, hold it for a pause, and let it out very slowly. "Thank you," I whisper, "thank you."

The social worker at the hospital is named Brittany, and her voice is so young and feminine, all I can imagine is Britney Spears on the other end of the phone as she gives me updates on my mom. "Pretty soon," Brittany coos, "her Medicare will be up and the hospital will discharge her. After that, she will have to pay out of pocket to stay in the hospital." Or, sometimes, it's about how she fell but didn't sustain any serious injuries. Or, it's about how we lost the appeal I filed to beg the hospital to keep her just a little longer until we could find a nursing home available. *Nothing* is available. Not one open bed in a nursing home in all of Western New York. How can this be?

When all the hope I have is completely gone, when the bucket of options and possibilities is bone dry, I call on Ganesha. Lord Ganesha is the beloved, Hindu elephant god who removes all obstacles in your life. Jesus and Mary are also beloved and seem to be experts in healing, courage and comfort. Ganesh is for chucking all the impossible, heavy shit aside. I send pleas from my tired, broken heart, mix in Om Gam Ganapataye Namaha about a thousand times, let the tears roll, and then thank him like he's a grandfather who just gave me a pony. It's an act of surrender to allow all the heartache and despair to pour out of you in an honest, intentional way. My tears become an offering. And it's never wasted. It works, every time. "Ganesh is fresh," says MC Yogi, and I know this to be true as well. I needed a miracle for my mom. There was nothing more I could do. I talked to social workers, lawyers, and free consultants who work for the Employee Assistance Program. I talked to therapists, financial advisors, doctors, nurses, and senior living consultants, Office of the Aging workers, family members, friends, the sky, anyone I could think of. There was one bed open back in Syracuse. My mom was going to be shipped to the largest, worst reviewed, dirtiest, and most neglectful nursing home in the state if we didn't get a miracle. The one-star reviews of this place said things like, "Don't send your loved ones here." I was terrified she would be sentenced there, but this was our only option. She was being discharged from the hospital.

All else had failed. So, I talked to Ganesha. I knew he could make miracles happen by lifting all the impossible things in my mom's path to a safer, better place to live, out of the hospital and to a place with more care. Brittany left me a message saying the hospital was preparing for discharge and that my mom would be going to Bishop Rehab in Syracuse the next morning. This was it, I told Ganesha, the wheels were in motion—it was now or never—I needed a miracle. I chanted a nonstop prayer to Ganesh and ignored my phone for the rest of the day. I just knew something better would come through.

The next morning, I received a call from Brittany telling us that a bed had opened up at Bishop Rehab in Syracuse where 451 other poor, elderly people were shipped due to the lack of availability anywhere else in Western New York. A place that was on the nightly news for medical malpractice and other violations regularly. A giant leap backwards, back toward the isolation of living on the farm, waiting to die. I did not answer my cell phone. I let Brittany leave her message, holding on to my miracle.

I realized that I'd been answering every phone call out of fear. I was afraid it meant that I didn't care if I didn't answer. I was afraid it meant that I was a terrible daughter if I didn't answer. I was afraid other people would decide my mom's fate if I didn't answer. But answering all the time was a full-time job that created a tightness in my chest, an invisible shake throughout my body, and pains in my heart. On this day, I ignored my phone and focused on being present for my students, steadying myself on a belief that our miracle would come. It had to. On this day, my tea tag read, "Be fearless; know that all will be provided at the right time."

On my lunch break, I sat down to rest and breathe a minute as twenty of my ten-year-old students hustled off to the cafeteria. My cell phone rang, and I answered it, holding my breath. It was Brittany telling me to ignore her previous message. We had an offer of a bed at the Elderwood Nursing Home in Hornell. Did we want that instead? *"Yes, we do!"* I shouted. I kept myself from saying, "I told you she was not going to Syracuse, that she would not go to that place." That omission was my kindness to her in that moment, for she was part of this miracle coming through at just the right time.

The next morning, Ada and I met my mom as she was delivered to Elderwood like a fragile, hand-delivered package only forty minutes from our home on Heron Hill. Finally, she was out of prison, she was safe. Thank you, Lord Ganesha. Thank you, God, Maker of Miracles, protector of my dreams. Thank you all. Thank you, beloved Universe. There is good at work, every moment. When I call upon it to rise up to work miracles, I am provided with just what I need, at the right time.

When I first came to the nursing home to meet my mom as they delivered her from the hospital, I was nervous. I feared all that I saw around me. Human beings that can no longer walk, sit up, or feed themselves. It was as if youth had been slowly sucked out of these people who were slumped over in chairs or draped sideways, lounging across recliners or asleep in wheelchairs in the middle of the day; sunshine streaming in from the windows went unnoticed. I tried to focus on my mom and the life that was still inside of her, to be grateful for all that the nurses, cleaners, and technicians were doing to take care of her and the other residents.

Upon my next visit to Elderwood, there was a power outage and a fire in the elevator. The nursing staff smelled smoke and pulled the fire alarm immediately. After going through the motions of hundreds of fire drills in schools and day care centers for the past twenty-five years, I knew we'd have to get everyone out of the building. I looked around at all the frail, elderly people draped over chairs and slumped in wheelchairs wondering how this was possible without an elevator. We were on the second floor of the building smelling smoke. I looked at a staff member and asked, "How can I help?"

As she deftly lifted an eighty-year-old man up from a chair she said, "We've got to get all the residents on the other side of those fire doors." She pointed, and I pushed my mom's wheelchair in that direction, noticing that no one else was moving.

It was the opposite of a school fire drill where everyone is out of the building in sixty-seconds flat. This was a slow-motion, no-panic, barely-audible-to-most fire alarm, and it was blasting away during an actual fire. With teamwork, we moved all the residents to the opposite side of the fire safety doors and waited for firefighters to arrive. In the meantime, my mom watched the others and waited patiently. I pulled out some hand lotion from my purse and rubbed some on her slender fingers as we talked.

Once everyone was settled, I watched the residents in wonder. They were all so different, and each so fascinating. The alarm was blaring, and I motioned for my mom to cover her ears with her fingers. I was calm. I was safe at that moment, as was my mom. So was Anna, and Hazel and Gertie and Elizabeth. So was the woman sitting beside me, running her fingertips along the surface of the table in front of her, repeatedly, like she was ice-skating with her hands. We'd made it! We'd all finally made it here safely, together. Another small miracle, I thought to myself, smiling.

Finally, the alarm sound was silenced as firefighters could be seen through the narrow windows of the doors. The fire was out, and repairs were underway. I had never experienced such a calm, slow emergency before this. It was fascinating and wonderful to watch everyone chat and shuffle about; to listen to my mom's fantastic tales once again. After the fire, after watching people with a sense of curiosity, my perspective shifted. I realized that I was seeing these elderly, dependent people through a lens of fear. I was afraid of becoming incapable and dependent on others myself; terrified of losing the last shreds of my youth, my physical strength, and abilities.

Now, when I visit, I say hello to people, and when my mom says, "This is my daughter, Kristin," I feel so grateful that she knows my name and wants to introduce me to someone else. When I asked one resident what her name was, she stared at me blankly. I asked again a bit louder thinking she might not be able to hear me. I noticed her hands were frozen in a stiff, arthritic position. I smiled as warmly as possible, making sure it showed through my eyes since the face mask was covering the lower half of my face.

Then, suddenly, I saw a slight smile come across her face and Craig, the maintenance man, called down the hallway, "Her name's Marie!"

"Hello, Marie, it's so nice to meet you."

Her smile filled her eyes, and she reached out to me. I clasped her hand in mine and saw the life, the love, and the youth inside her beaming out. We connected there for one beautiful moment before we walked to another room for lunchtime.

During another visit, I sat and watched my mom eat her ham and scalloped potatoes, green beans, and milk served on a large tray. She told me about how they were experimenting with urine spray on the food there just to see if they would notice. She told me they didn't give her any medicine today and that she was very busy and had been out doing errands earlier and that the roads were awful. She told me my father had gotten taller and that he was dating someone new. She said he told her that he knew he wasn't supposed to, but that he was putting himself on "The Singles List" anyway and maybe he'd see her there.

As I listened to the latest tall-tales, I watched two nursing home technicians tend to an elderly man who appeared to be frozen in a recliner, his chin lifted, his hands curled in like dead leaves. They spoke to him softly, gently brushing the hair out of his eyes, helping him transfer to a chair to eat his lunch, placing a large, terry-cloth bib over his shirt. Instead of seeing this man with fear and resistance, all I could see now was the compassion and connection given and received in this daily interaction. It was beautiful and helped me accept that indeed, this is my fate. I will lose my youth, my strength, my physical and mental abilities. I may rely on others to care for me, and when that day comes, I hope I send love and gratitude toward those who lovingly help me eat my lunch.

Henry & Dan

"When you do things from your soul, you feel
a river moving in you, a joy." — Rumi

Henry. Hen-hen. Prince Henry. Henry Mancini. Pumpernickel. My dearest, closest friend for fourteen years was a chocolate lab named Henry. Our School Resource Officer, Josh Galen, raised Labrador Retrievers and was known locally for having beautiful, loyal family dogs. One day while I was running an elementary art class, Josh came through the halls with a large cardboard box filled with puppies. I refused to investigate said box every time it was offered. It felt like birth control. I was being smart. *Don't look in the box, and for God's sake don't pick one up.* Then, it would be all over, and I'd have a baby on my hands.

Several weeks later, Officer Galen was making his rounds with the cardboard box again when I had an exceptionally harmonious kindergarten class. "Last two puppies if you wanna take a look," he said grinning. He was guessing he'd broken me down enough, and he was right: I peeked over the side of the box. In the corner was a tiny, round ball of dark chocolate velvet with giant eyes and a whimper. At that moment, my thinking brain switched off and my hands scooped up the chocolate ball and pulled it to my chest. I breathed in deeply through my nose, inhaling puppy elixir. Instantly, it was over. My life was forever changed at that moment.

When I called Chad to ask if we could have a dog, he said, "Yes, bring him home!" Henry was still too young to come home with us, but after that day, he was ours. I picked him up a week later and drove home with him whining on my lap like a kidnapped baby.

Dan, on the other hand, was much harder to come by. It'd been over two years after Chad and I divorced when I found myself on my knees in front of the mural I'd painted of the Holy Mother Mary, begging for help, sobbing, and swearing that I was ready to move on with my life. Om Sri Matre Namaha became my daily chant, followed by as many Hail-Mary prayers I could repeat, on my knees. I didn't care that I blended disparate religions—I needed a team! I needed a loving, supportive mother who had the strength and courage to see my pain, to stay with me through it, and to befriend me as a single parent. I felt so alone, so lost, for so long. I felt alone in my marriage for so many years that it felt like I'd spent a decade or more alone, longing for a partner; dreaming of someone who wanted to spend time with me, to share life together, to witness one another's existence, to walk together. I was always walking Henry alone, or with a baby strapped to my back. I was ready to move on with my life. I'd accepted Chad and Laura's relationship, that ours was dead, or at least, it had transformed into co-parenting with grace and patience. I wanted to meet someone who was healthy and happy, someone who cared for themselves so well they could also care for me, Ada, and Henry. I spent several hours chanting, praying, and meditating one night when I felt fortified, strong, and ready. "I'm ready," I repeated to the Universe, to Mary, "I'm ready, I'm ready. I'm ready!"

The next morning, my Aunt Sandy called and told me she had a friend she really wanted me to meet, and his name was Dan. Somehow, I felt this was the Mother of the Universe saying, "Well, you asked, so here you go! Here is the perfect partner for you, my child."

Aunt Sandy always loved to create clay sculptures in her free time and continues to take classes at our local art center in her retirement from nursing. Dan was in her class making sculptures himself. "What's your lady situation, Dan?" asked the retired ladies surrounding him in the basement of the art center, up to their elbows in clay. "Uh...I don't have one," he answered. After that Aunt Sandy hounded me to meet Dan. She left messages, she even pulled over when she drove by while I was out walking Henry. "When are you going to meet *Dan*?" She'd repeat this mantra for nearly a month before I finally decided to reach out and contact him. I knew this must be a gift from the universe, but for some reason, I didn't allow myself to believe it. Not until the day I met Dan in person. When he introduced himself and talked about his life, he included, of course, that he had a son, that he was an elementary school teacher, a track coach, and...a caretaker. Dan and his son lived in some sort of historic house as the caretaker. I knew by the end of our first date that he was the one for me.

When I first met Dan, I did not recognize him. It was drizzling rain and already dark on a March evening in Alfred, NY. We met at the coffee house and shared a meal and some good conversation. By the end of the date, while he introduced me to his Prius hybrid electric, I suddenly recognized him. It was a felt experience of knowing this man for centuries, as if we'd been together for millennia. His fingertips touched down on the hood of the little, red car like a rover landing on mars. I felt it in my bloodstream, a vibration was sent through my entire body in that moment. This man is my *partner*! "Can I use the phone number your aunt gave me?" he called out as I crossed the street to leave. "Sure," I said.

Dan and I had been dating for about a year when moving in together was first mentioned. Ada was six, Henry was twelve, and Dan's son, Riley, was going on thirteen when we first became a family. Dinners and game nights, movies and restaurants, long walks with Henry and lots of talking shaped this new tribe. "We have plenty of room in the Pinkhouse," he smirked. It was no surprise to find out that Dan was an *actual caretaker*—he lived in the historic Pinkhouse in Wellsville for about four years at that time, and he'd taken me on an unofficial tour during one of our first dates. I marveled at all the stained-glass windows, and of course, there was a floor to ceiling tapestry featuring a Great Blue Heron. I froze in front of the tapestry covering the wall of the dining room. My spirit guide winked at me, I swear, and although I didn't want to move from that spot, I took my time wandering through the rest of the old house, listening to Dan's extensive knowledge about its history.

After a few first dates we decided that it was important to introduce Riley and Ada to one another, because if that didn't go well it was simply a deal-breaker. I came with a smelly old chocolate lab and a six-year-old daughter, period. Dan came with a twelve-year-old son, and much later I found out, a Ball Python named Rocky, and a Harley Davidson, but that's another story.

One thing I loved about Dan immediately was that he did not play any head games. There was no toying around trying to make the other person like them or trying to feign interest or play it cool. He liked me and he showed me, straight up. When we gathered the kids around my kitchen table to play board games, he would pull my chair as close as possible to his chair and press the side of his leg into mine just to feel me next to him. It was honest and beautiful, and the kids adored each other. There were some nights when I focused on meeting someone who took such good care of themselves that they could also, lovingly, willingly, take care of me and Ada too. And here he was. Dan, the runner, the teacher, the track coach, the *caretaker*. He had arrived in my life with perfect tim-

Henry following Dan up to the Pine St. property
& Henry at the Pinkhouse, Wellsville, NY

ing, a loving heart, a sharp mind, and a warmth I'd dreamed of for years. Dan and I continued to see each other a few times a week for over a year when Ada, Henry, and I decided to move, this time, with joy, into the Pinkhouse in Wellsville with Dan, Riley, and Rocky (the snake).

We moved from our spacious, four-bedroom house in Almond to share a bedroom with Dan, a closet with Ada, and a bathroom between the four of us. It was close quarters in what I lovingly called the "side pocket" of the Pinkhouse, which was actually an apartment added on for the family's in-laws during the 1920s. We adjusted to living closely together and made some wonderful memories there as Riley became a senior in high school and Ada a middle-school student. At this point, Henry was arthritic and old, preferred myself and Dan exclusively but settled into living at the Pinkhouse rather nicely.

One morning, Henry couldn't make it up the ten porch steps to get back in the house after his morning constitution in the yard. I helped him up the steps and he lay sprawled out on the floor, refusing to eat or drink. That's when I knew he was in trouble. I called in sick and secured a substitute for school, even though there weren't any to be had. My principal had to cover my classes, which she was not happy about, but something in me knew this could be Henry's last day with us.

It was a struggle to carry him into the house, but I got him inside, made him comfortable, and sat close to him until his last breaths came in great waves, letting me know he was leaving this world. The body of my closest, most loyal companion for fourteen years lay motionless on the floor as

I held him, feeling him leave this world, and allowing myself to enter a new realm of grief. I held him close, thanking him, telling him how much I loved him. Then, he was gone. Henry had one bad day, and left this world with ease. I sobbed over his dead body for hours until Dan and the kids came home from school and said their goodbyes.

Henry immediately loved Dan upon meeting him and let me know he'd follow him anywhere. He trusted Dan fully and loved every moment he got to spend with us. Hen hated when Dan was on the tractor, which happened a lot when we were getting the Pine Street property ready for a house. If Dan was up on that orange Kubota, Henry was barking at him to "get off, immediately." I'd have to drag him away so he was at a safe distance as Dan excavated and shaped the roadway.

After Henry died, we talked about where he might be or what form he might possibly take. Henry brought so much love, devotion, and companionship to my life for fourteen years, that I felt his absence acutely.

As Dan was working on the tractor the next day, a large crow landed in a nearby tree and cawed at him incessantly. This happened for several days in a row, and we believed it to be Henry, still telling him to get off that terrifying machine. Eventually, after many months, I was able to let Henry go. He'd already left our lives together, so my heart and mind had some catching up to do. I pulled over after delivering Ada to her dad for the weekend and sat along a babbling brook, my heart heavy with grief. Listening to the sounds of nature, I was soon overcome with a sense that Henry was there with me, enjoying the beauty and peace of this little spot I'd discovered. I prayed to know if he was safe, if he was okay, wherever he was. I removed my shoes and began to walk through the cold water. I stepped onto a small island of tall grasses and rocks, carefully exploring nature in its spring colors. As I stepped again, I looked down to see a nest directly beneath me and froze. A large egg sat snug inside, full of speckles, and I was filled with delight at the potential of new life. *New life!* There was my answer, staring back at me, and I remembered Henry the crow. He's free now, so I had better be as well.

We celebrated three fantastic Halloweens at the Pinkhouse together, when hundreds of local kids came to the mansion's large front doors in costume, tingling with excitement. We waited out Covid-19 there together, through all its ups and downs, and Henry passed away on the living room floor in my arms. The silver lining around this time in my life was building a beautiful partnership and friendship with Dan. He let me weep and held me lovingly until I was ready to smile and laugh again. I'm so grateful he's still by my side today.

After the Storm, acrylic, Kristin Buchholz, 2020

Remembering Henry, acrylic, Kristin Buchholz, 2020

The Pinkhouse: Wellsville, NY

"I love life so much that I never want to die." — E.B. Hall

The first time I slept over at the historic, Victorian house in Wellsville locally known as the "Pinkhouse," I dreamt there were dragons circling overhead, breathing fire, descending on the castle. I vaguely remember lying flat on my back on a cold stone floor, looking up through the great windows of a vaulted ceiling. As the breathing of three enormous, black dragons intensified, the warmth of their flames was felt on my face, and I became terrified. "Hot air balloon," I heard Dan whisper. "What?" I questioned, without

opening my eyes. "Come on, get up, there are hot air balloons above us!" Dan repeated with more urgency as he hopped into his pajama pants one leg at a time. Hair and glasses askew, PJ's and sweaters pulled on frantically, we arrived in the front yard of the Pinkhouse to find a hot air balloon sailing slowly through the morning sky. We waved, excitedly.

This explains the dragons, I thought to myself, listening to the fire rush into the balloon that continued its descent.

The tiny people in the basket waved back at us. Once within earshot, they began talking to us, hovering steadily. "What are they saying?" I asked. Dan looked at me and shrugged. In another minute or two the giant balloon was directly overhead, and we heard more clearly, "Can we have permission to land here?" "Yes, you sure can!" Dan shouted into the sky. Slowly, this enormous hot-air balloon landed in the front yard of the Pinkhouse just as it might have a century ago. We grabbed a hold of giant ropes as they were tossed out of the basket and followed orders from the aeronautic crew as they emerged from their ship. They tethered the airship and gave us rides high into the sky so we could see the grand estate from above as the birds do. We shared the traditional bottle of champagne with the family of balloonists at eight o'clock in the morning and helped pack up their equipment into a small trailer pulled behind their Subaru. Every moment of my life has been magical after meeting Dan. This day just took the cake.

Most Wellsvillians believe the Pinkhouse is haunted. Nearly everyone we talked to about living there asked, "So, …is it *haunted?*" People are not that interested in the truth in this situation. They want a story to share. They want to go home and tell their families that they spoke with the caretakers of the Pinkhouse and you'll never guess what happens in that place…When honestly, I'm sorry to say, no, it's not haunted. It's just a big, empty house that's stuck in time. Nearly all the furniture, the paintings, the art, the light fixtures (they'd been converted from gas to electric) remained the same as they were over a hundred and fifty years ago. There was one thing, though…

In 1907, there was a circular water fountain in the front yard, complete with potted urns and life-size swans made of zinc that floated lazily. Much like the romantic scenes E.B. Hall and his wife Antoinette witnessed on their honeymoon travels in Venice, Italy. As one story goes, their daughter Fannie left the house to walk to the mailbox and may have left one of the heavy front doors ajar. Two-year old Beatrice, E.B. Hall's grandchild wandered out and down the front steps to the fountain, perhaps attracted to the swans. She may have tripped and hit her head, toppling into the fountain. Her mother returned from the mailbox to find her beautiful baby girl face down in the water of the fountain. Fannie screamed for help and doctors arrived, but all attempts to revive the little girl failed. This was long before mouth to mouth resuscitation was developed in 1956. "Mr. Hall was seated on the front porch but confined to a wheelchair and was unable to be of assistance in saving his granddaughter's life." This tragedy has never left the family of the historic Pinkhouse, and a portrait of beautiful Beatrice still hangs in the drawing room today. The fountain and swans are gone, however, as the grieving family removed them soon after their daughter died within their depths. The story found its way into books about houses that were haunted, which fueled local legends about the Pinkhouse that persist today. One of the most frequent questions Dan got as caretaker was, "Is it haunted?" His response was always, "no, sorry to tell you, it's not."

After E.B. Hall died in 1908, his wife Antoinette in 1917,

and their son J. Milton Carpenter in 1926, his daughter Florence (Beatrice's older sister) lived away from home, leaving Fannie Hall Carpenter alone in the Pinkhouse with a housekeeper. It was then decided "…to convert several rooms on the west side of the house into a caretaker's apartment, which has remained so ever since." I don't know how many caretakers, housekeepers, landscapers, cooks, or staff lived or worked for the E.B. Hall dynasty, but the love of my life was one of them. Interestingly enough, nothing is written about the people who cared for the historic house or its grounds, only the wealthy family members who occupied its rooms. When Dan and his son Riley Allen lived there from 2014 to 2020, they helped a housekeeper, landscaping crew, and groundskeeper take care of the property. It was part of Dan's contract that he would take care of removing all fallen leaves on the property when the time came each autumn and remove snow from the driveway and sidewalks flanking the property along West State and South Brooklyn. Before leaving to teach at Wellsville elementary, Dan would bundle up from head to toe to shovel and occasionally run the snow-blower, clearing driveway and sidewalks before sunrise. We often worked together to rake autumn leaves onto tarps and drag them to the curb where city workers came to haul them away.

When Ada and I joined Dan and Ry at the Pinkhouse, my dear friend Jody mentioned the popular TV series Downton Abbey, which I had never seen. I thought about all the workers who'd been there before us, their toil and labor undocumented, their work unappreciated. When I chopped vegetables and prepared dinner in the tiny caretaker's kitchen, I thought about the cooks and housekeepers from the past, the invisible work of the poor, women, and people of color who must have toiled away in this very spot, standing on this black and white checkered floor.

One way to enter the main house from our apartment was to pass through a small broom closet that connected the two spaces. Our home, "the side pocket," as I called it, was warm and well-lit, full of art and living plants, piles of shoes, kids' toys, video games, bunk beds and musical instruments. When you entered the broom closet, there was a wall of wooden shelves and cupboards filled with pink and white tea sets; a mop with a long, worn wooden handle painted pink hung on the inside of the door. Teacups hung delicately on brass hooks. Everything was tidy and in place, still and silent. Closing the door behind left you in darkness for a moment, so you could pull the long metal chain to switch on the light above, or just have the key ready to unlock the second door that led into the kitchen of the Pinkhouse. Usually, I had the light on, the key ready and music playing. I wanted everyone, in any dimension, to know where I was going.

We often checked on leaks, cracks in the walls, noisy plumbing, thermostat readings and the like, or Dan did, I should say, although I explored the place many times myself, for various reasons. Sometimes one of the other caretakers would leave something important on the kitchen table for us to move, take care of or put away. There was always something to do with a house this old. It needed lots of attention. I was mildly curious if the house was indeed haunted and wanted to find out for myself.

I got permission from Dan to have a small scavenger hunt through the house for one of Ada's birthday parties and needed to set it up. I wrote clues on pink slips of paper, leading the kids through the house and up to the tower where I left dozens of pink balloons for them to find. The floorboards creaked, the carpeted stairs groaned a bit, but I never sensed any apparitions, only large, empty rooms that held untold stories of many past lives. Along the hallway upstairs, an entire wall is filled with black and white portraits of the many generations of E.B. Hall's family. Edwin Bradford Hall, descendant of William Bradford Hall, a Puritan Separatist who traveled to America on the Mayflower and later became Governor of Plymouth Colony. From E.B. and Antoinette to the people we talked to today, their great, great-grandson Jay Woelfel and his wife, Christy, who live in California and visit the house a few times a year. I loved looking at the faces of all these people who'd lived in this very house, who'd walked down this very hallway, slept in these beds, and washed in these tubs. I gave them my attention and respect, thanking them for having been here before us. Yet none of them talked back to me, knocked any books off shelves or smashed any dishes like self-respecting ghosts might. It was just quiet and still, peaceful and calm, a bit sad, perhaps. "The Hall-Carpenter family never fully recovered from the tragic death of baby Beatrice." I wondered if there was still grief and sadness in the house when we were living happily in its side-pocket, full of life and color.

When we lived in the Pinkhouse, the busiest, most stressful times were right before the family was scheduled to visit.

Vicky and Susan worked tirelessly getting the house ready: cleaning and pulling out decorations, linens, towels and the

like. Dan had to make sure plumbing and heating was ready, and once Vicky told Dan there was a bat in the basement, he needed to take care of. We were not allowed to park in the front circle, only out back near the carriage house so the family could park out front and come and go as they pleased. We needed to have all the work done and remain invisible, a bit like the staff at Downton Abbey, working away in the kitchens down below the castle, hustling about silently behind the scenes. Although I didn't do much but help Dan with raking or shoveling, I just imagined that I was somehow connected to the staff who occupied these spaces a hundred years ago. These times were infrequent, and mostly, the Pinkhouse was our home. We just occupied a small slice of it, feeling the empty rooms of the rest looming over us. It had no insulation, was very cold and drafty everywhere, no matter how much we heated it. Ada and I shared a small closet and, during the winter months, if you didn't take your clothes out of it the night before, they'd be too stiff and cold to put on in the morning. The four of us shared the caretaker's apartment with the tiny kitchen and one bathroom for three years before we bought the vacant plot of land just around the corner on Pine Street.

The year before we left, I paused to notice Ada, as we

were about to walk Henry around the block. She was dressed head to toe in pink. I swore that I'd never make her conform to gender norms, give her barbies, or make her wear pink. She was going to be her own person. And at that moment, pink helmet clipped in place, pink T-shirt and striped skirt, sandals, and pink scooter, she was nothing like I'd expected, posing in front of the Pinkhouse. "Surprise!" Life seemed to be saying to me—no matter how hard you tried to resist, here it is, this Pink in all its glory, my little girl vibrant, safe and healthy. How could I be anything less than grateful?

We'd just had an Easter egg hunt and invited many friends from Ada's class to explore the gardens surrounding the house. The tall Hickories and Hemlocks sheltered so much wildlife that the squirrels and chipmunks broke into many brightly colored plastic eggs before our guests had even arrived. It was loads of fun anyway, and I was so grateful the Woelfel's allowed us to do such things while we lived there.

Marcile Woelfel was such a delightful, kind-hearted woman. Married to Julian Woelfel, who grew up in the Pinkhouse, and a descendant of E.B. Hall, Marcile adored the Pinkhouse, its history and everything about it. When she visited, she usually had cleaning and sorting projects, entertained guests and had many visitors. One tradition Marcile practiced was to leave the lamp on in the large bay windows of the house to let neighbors know she was home. We would never pass through the broom closet and emerge into the kitchen to visit her when she came. We left the house, walked all the way around and up the steps to the porch on the opposite side of the mansion to ring the doorbell like all her other visitors. She was warm and hospitable, sharing stories and conversation every time. At the age of ninety, she was independent and still driving, visiting from Ohio where she resided alone after her husband Julian passed away. Shortly after, she moved into an assisted living community and had long-time housekeeper Vicky travel to Ohio to drive her back to Wellsville for visits.

When Marcile passed away, we too were ready to leave the Pinkhouse, but we knew it wasn't time to tell the Woelfel's yet. The family held a lovely ceremony in Marcile's honor on the front lawn. Folding chairs lined the yard, facing the house where family members like her sons Jay and Jack spoke from the front porch. The Pinkhouse itself seemed like an imposing family member, larger than life, standing up straight to honor Marcile. Marcile adored Wellsville and their family's Pinkhouse tradition and gave us Pinkhouse ornaments, cards and even a children's book about living in Wellsville that featured the famous Victorian home. When Marcile sent Dan Christmas cards from Ohio, she used to sign it, with love, from the Pinkhouse.

The four of us were tucked away in the caretaker's apartment during the global pandemic from the spring of 2019 through the summer of 2020. Surprisingly enough, Marcile eventually gave me permission to lead some Yoga classes in the lush, green yards of the house during summer months. Luckily, we had the outdoor spaces that felt like a much greater refuge than the side pocket, and we developed a regular tradition of feeding the squirrels and chipmunks with peanuts. Crows, blue jays, cardinals and even an occasional red-tailed hawk (swooping after a chipmunk) joined in for the feeding adventures. The squirrels became so accustomed to us they would walk slowly, with curiosity to just a few feet away until we tossed a peanuty treat. One May it snowed. Not just a light dusting that melts away by afternoon, either, but several inches that stuck around for a couple of days. I decided then and there it was reason enough to develop a new tradition. Whenever it snows in May, from here on out, we will celebrate "Merry May!" I had a feeling that if we didn't do something fun and spontaneous, this just might break us. "Quick, everyone, find or make something into a gift to give. No money spent, just creativity and time…go!" After about an hour we gathered on the family room floor with snacks and our Charlie-Brown gifts. I got the best pair of alpaca wool socks I've ever felt on my feet and Ada got a creepy doll-art sculpture from Dan. We turned the uninvited inclement weather into some joyful memories, and I'm so grateful we had that time together at the Pinkhouse.

Eventually, we told the Woelfels that we had a new home waiting for us just around the corner and that we were ready to go. We agreed to continue to check on Pink and take care of the autumn leaves while they searched for a new caretaker. We recommended someone and before long, their new hire was moving in and we were moving up.

During two previous summers, Dan used the orange Kubota tractor he traded for his Harley, to shape a road and drainage ditches that stretched 740 feet from Pine Street into the overgrown pasture to where we wanted our future house to be. We thought maybe we'd build the house ourselves but started with the barn first. While living in the Pinkhouse, Dan used all his spare time up at the Pine Street Property. He'd leave me notes that read, "Off to work at PSP" (Pine Street Property) until that's what we called it. It took all summer to build the barn on PSP, and the next summer to dig all the drainage ditches. Dan dug deep to bury the water and sewage lines and got into the mud himself to lay the pipe. Day after day, he did the same thing. He dug with the tractor scoop, jumped into the hole, laid PVC pipe, glued it together, then covered it back up with dirt. Every day for an entire summer. Sweating in the mud, day in and day out. We watched the movie Ground Hog's Day that summer because Dan kept saying that his life kept repeating over and over again with the same thing every day. Until one glorious day, when it was complete. Water lines, electric and fiber optic cables were all buried in the ground along the gravel road that led into the property, leaving you at a clearing with a lovely view of distant hills and Wellsville's Main Street. We took family and friends up to see this empty little spot and enjoy the view for many months. We took Ada and Riley up to have campfires and imagine how our new home would look right in that spot. Ada inspired a new tradition for our family Christmas when she sobbed and wrapped herself into a hug on the stump of a tree we'd cut down to bring a Christmas tree back to the Pinkhouse. She said nothing, but cried and mourned the life we'd taken. And she was right. From then on, we bought potted evergreen trees and planted them on the property in the early spring. This became our first family tradition for our new home, which had not yet arrived. Until one day, in July of 2020, just before building supplies were gone and so many industries shut down due to the pandemic, our house was delivered.

The bank would not approve a loan for us to build it ourselves, since we weren't certified contractors, so we spent two years looking at modular homes that were built inside huge factories. Owl Homes in Olean was the closest place to us to tour these homes, and we even went to the factory in Pennsylvania to see how they were built. It was an exciting, impressive operation and we were ready to buy. Eventually we found just the right home and watched it fly through the air, held with a crane, and set into place right on the spot we chose. The same spot where we had campfires, walked with Henry, and explored with the kids. We watched the house get lowered expertly into place, one piece at a time; the crew zoomed around attaching, hammering, fixing it all in place. It was like watching a human beehive at work until the house was done. We were simply in awe that we could have hoped for, prayed for, and imagined such a thing happening and then got to watch it come true.

We had chosen the perfect spot for our new home but couldn't move in for a few more months yet. The more we came to visit, the more herons we began to notice. Directly over the house, Great Blue Herons flew from their nesting grounds out to Alma Pond or the Genesee River to fish and back home to their nests. We were making our home directly beneath the sky path of the Great Blue Herons. This was not just the perfect spot for us to start our lives together, but a sacred place I'd been guided to over many decades. Looking for signs, making small pivots as I navigated life's perplexing labyrinth, searching for truth, for a belief that we are not alone through this earth walk, but loved, supported and guided every step of the way.

175 Pine

"You belong to life. With love and reverence, you will find the peace and harmony of this." — Akal Pritam

"I don't think of all the misery, but of the beauty that still remains." — Anne Frank

Roughly a century ago, 175 Pine Street had a small house, a barn or small carriage house out back, and a family who lived in and around them with about eleven acres of pasture land out back. The pasture may have had cows or horses on it, but along the edge of this property ran a pipeline owned by the Sinclair Oil Refinery. In the early 1800s, Whitesville, Wellsville, Allentown, and the Bolivar-Richburg areas (the Southern-tier of western New York, as we call it) experienced an oil boom where significant quantities of oil were discovered, and land was bought up from farmers by eager investors. There was suddenly an abundance of jobs besides farming and teaching, by golly! The Sinclair Oil Refinery built a sizable brick factory along the Genesee River, and it sits empty, crumbling there still today. Back then, they needed all kinds of pipes and convenient ways to dump waste and such. A long, rusted pipe can be found along the southern edge of 175 Pine, which, oddly enough, heads straight downhill toward the old Sinclair Refinery.

As I walked the property lines today, I swept through tall grasses along what's often a muddy path that most of the year is flooded or gushing with spring water. My dad taught me how to identify a Poplar, so I stopped as I approached the grove of Poplars, looking up. Their spade-shaped leaves look like they're waving at you in the wind. I often feel compelled to stop and wave back. Suddenly, a young fawn leaped out of the tall grass before me. I froze with a gasp as I watched her spotted, pebble-shaped body bound away frantically. I know this fawn, and I'm surprised she doesn't remember me. Or perhaps she does.

The first time we met she was curled up on the shoulder of the gravel road Dan formed with his Kubota tractor. Our road leads up to where we're planning to have the house delivered from Owl Homes, in the next year or two. She was in a warm, sunny spot as I drove up one night. I thought maybe Dan had dropped his brown sweatshirt off the back of the tractor while driving up this steeper section of driveway. I slowed to a halt and got out of the Nissan.

As soon as I approached, I saw it was not a sweatshirt, but a fawn. A teeny, tiny, curled up fawn, possibly just days old, resting in the sunshine. Her speckles were decent camouflage, but in the fading light the gravel drive shone a cold gray where she looked like a warm, toasted marshmallow. I spoke to her softly and called up to Dan. I refused to drive by her, which might make her startle or leap headfirst into the vehicle.

Dan sauntered downhill, annoyed that he had to stop his work building the barn farther up the hillside, but when I pointed her out, he settled gently into the man I know and love. I expressed my worry that I could hurt her driving by, and he directed me, so I'd know I wasn't too close as I crept by like a snail up the rest of the hillside. As I helped Dan build the second story of the barn that afternoon, I checked on her regularly. I could see her, shaded and alone, still in a ball on the edge of the road. The second or third check showed me she was indeed alive, as she had lifted her head with a long, graceful neck, apparently looking for mama.

When our stomachs told us it was time for dinner, we crept past her in the Nissan once again, hoping she would be okay and that it wouldn't be too cold in the dark and that mama would come scoop her up before nightfall. Thankfully, when we returned in the morning to work on the barn, she was gone.

It was completely by accident that I discovered this fawn's twin earlier that afternoon. As we worked throughout the day, I eventually had to pee in the grass then head downhill to work on planting some trees. I didn't want to frighten the fawn, still curled up on the roadside, so I walked through the tall grass and buckthorn on the other side of the ditch along the road, giving her a wide berth hoping she and mama deer, wherever she was hiding, would feel safe. Yet, as I swept long, quiet steps through the tall grass and blue forget-me-nots, another fawn lay in hiding. This one, however, was at least twice as big and laying like a puppy ready to play, front legs outstretched. Her nose was enormous and reminded me of my beloved Henry's chocolate brown nose. I stepped slowly around her, offering reassuring tones and noticed her gaze was averted. As if her mother had warned just that morning,

"Do not look into the eye of the great white beast."

Mama deer showed herself unwittingly several times that afternoon, apparently keeping watch on both her babies, bounding between the two, negotiating Human predators all the while. We figured they were fraternal twins, as is common for White-tailed deer in springtime. They must have been just days old then. My encounter with one of the twins earlier today suggests that they are now a few weeks old, having gained strength in their gangly legs, leaping, and creeping about our eleven-acre plot, balancing freedom and security as summer begins. This is how our lives at 175 Pine Street begin.

As I walk around the edges of our property, our new home, I marvel at how I got here, at all the moving and searching I've done in this lifetime. I pause and tune into the sounds of the wind and nearby bird calls. I return to my blissful childhood before all the heartbreak and say thank you to whoever is listening, to the sky above and the ground below. Nearly 49 years old, I wonder where the time has gone. Later, I leaf through an old journal and find this:

I've given my youth
to the meadow.
With each breath it's
grown up into Queen Anne's Lace
and honey-scented Goldenrod.
I've given my youth
to the trail.
With each step it's
returned with blackberry brambles

and Honeysuckle roses.
I've given my youth
to the forest.
With every season its elders
have whispered wisdom and
comfort that heals old hurts.
I've given my youth
to the country.
With every new day
it rises with bold color
or the winking moon
before it fades into the Great Blue.

9/16/22

A Home on Heron Hill

"Sorrow prepares you for joy. It violently sweeps everything out of your house, so that new joy can find space to enter. It shakes the yellow leaves from the bough of your heart, so that fresh, green leaves can grow in their place. It pulls up the rotten roots, so that new roots hidden beneath have room to grow. Whatever sorrow shakes from your heart, far better things will take their place." — Rumi

It is a frigid December evening nearly two years after this global pandemic began, and both Dan and I have tested positive for Covid-19. We were careful, wearing masks everywhere all day teaching at school and anywhere out in public, washing our hands until they were raw. We were fully vaccinated months ago and even received a booster shot just weeks ago. I felt terrible taking a third vaccination when most of the world's population, my extended family, has not even had one dose. But it was recommended, and we planned to have family over for Christmas, so it seemed like the responsible thing to do. I urged anyone who was not vaccinated to get a test before they came over. My dear cousin, Alysia, was having some cold symptoms but didn't think it was anything unusual, nor did I. After spending three days with us, her symptoms worsened, and she took a test. Positive for Covid-19. I took one myself and I was also positive, Dan too. We had already had most of the family over for dinner just days ago. We called them all, urging them once again to get tested, apologizing profusely. I feel okay, well enough, but Dan is not well. He's feverish, aching, and dizzy. He's coughing violently, and I'm sneezing a lot, feeling underwater. We are holed up here in our new home on Heron Hill, hoping to heal together. Tonight, I kneeled with Buddha, praying for everyone suffering from illness, loss and grief, to be healed, and then I settled in to write some more.

Surely the grief I walked through for two years after leaving Chad shook loose much of what I needed to shed. Surely, this joyful life with Dan that continues to grow, and blossom is not over so soon. We have acres of buckthorn to uproot, new trees to plant, a garage and chicken coop to build. "We have plans, for crying out loud, big plans. Please, help us." The prayers leak out of my chest like sweat and I know they need not form into words to be understood. As my symptoms worsened, I got a text from Chad that Ada was also positive and that I needed to come get her, ASAP. Laura's entire family was coming up from North Carolina, they'd just arrived in fact, and I needed to take her, immediately. As I lay in bed drowning in phlegm, I formulated a plan to pull myself together enough to make the three-hour, round-trip drive. A shower and change of clothing helped, and I returned home safely with a very sick child.

Not only were her symptoms worse than mine, but also, her heart was broken. She was just kicked out of a house decked out for Christmas, dishes simmering, snacks piling up, gifts wrapped, lights twinkling, only to be removed from the festivities. She was devastated. Her hopes for Christmas joy were slashed open like gaudy wrapping paper, only to reveal fever, cough, congestion, and headache. For the next three days the three of us stuck it out in our own little corners of the house, gathering for meals (since we were all sick together anyway) and some gift exchanges. We managed to make merry on Christmas day and turned a corner, symptoms waning, white blood cells kicking Covid's ass. Fear, be gone! We will survive this, together.

When the four of us lived in the Pinkhouse, we watched spring intentionally unfold over weeks and weeks as winter gave in to her sun rays. That first spring we were all sent home from school, fumbling through online schooling, someone had the liberal idea to create a very forgiving "At-home school day schedule," which broke up the day into hourly periods of exercise, reading, journaling, outside time, lunch, math, science and creative activities. It allowed us more time to look out the windows and notice what was going on in our own backyards. We watched wildlife cautiously creep into grassy knolls as tree buds fattened. We filled bird feeders together, fed squirrels and chipmunks and noticed a gentle rhythm form as spring flourished. Eventually, we realized that it was good and safe to spend time outside. Our fear slowly fell away like brown oak leaves, and we relaxed enough to notice tiny, yellow-green buds and wildflowers in the yard. Once, a red-tailed hawk swooped just inches past my right shoulder, zeroing in on a chipmunk I was feeding. It missed, as the little racer dove into its tunnel home.

Not everyone was so lucky. Covid-19 has killed so many

people, severed so many connections, and broke so many hearts. I've been to several memorial services and missed many more because it was too dangerous to gather so many people together in one, indoor place. In our small school, many teachers and students remained unvaccinated for various reasons, some of which were misinformation and lies. When Ada began fifth grade at the start of the next school year, I was finally her art teacher. I felt like I'd been waiting for this since she'd been born. Instead of going to school together, however, Ada stayed home and I was made to teach my art classes alone in my classroom in front of a computer screen. Everything was upside down. My dear friend, Cindi, made an enormous painting years ago that I think of now. She painted the word "Believe" in a beautiful blue with the "-lie" part of the word in red. There is a bald face lie right in the center of this beautiful word, Believe. Cindi painted this after she discovered that her husband had been cheating on her with another woman for over a year.

No one really knows what to believe anymore, so we just choose. We choose where we want to belong and with whom—I'm with you, so that's what I will believe. I trust doctors, nurses, healthcare workers and paramedics, nursing home attendants, aides, technicians, and scientists far more than politicians, especially when it comes to medical advice, so I choose to believe them. I take their truths along with their lies, their hopes along with their failures. I choose to focus on healing, survival, and compassion. As Brene Brown writes in Atlas of the Heart, "Science is not the truth. Science is finding the truth. When science changes its opinion, it didn't lie to you. It learned more."

When Julia died, no one knew what to believe. She did have Covid-19, if you believe the tests, but she seemed better. She was back at school teaching, just like the rest of us. She went to Florida briefly to visit her daughter who was accepted to the Delta training program for new pilots. She was so very proud of her daughter and three sons. Her heart was so full. She poured love into her students just like she did her own children. And then suddenly, she was gone.

Today and yesterday, I sat with four different middle school classes whose teacher passed away. We all arrived back at school Monday morning to hear the news that our dear friend and co-teacher had died the night before. She was 54 years old and a mother of four. Julia Deichmann was planning to retire next year. She and her husband, a kind, intelligent dairy farmer, had bought a camper the summer before, making plans to travel. Julia had the most beautiful smile and such a kind and loving way about her. She loved her students just like she loved her own children; with a depth and clarity that always put their best interests first.

Her fifth-grade students were informed of her passing by guidance counselors and soon after came to my room for art class. I sat them all together around a large, oval table just to help us see each other and connect for a few minutes. We began with a mindfulness of sounds practice for a minute or two and took some deep breaths before I shared how I was feeling. The moments of quiet helped ground me in the present moment before acknowledging the difficult emotions we were all feeling.

I shared how hard this was to feel such loss and pain, to not be able to say goodbye. As I was naming some feelings, I could feel tension in my chest that rose to my throat, making it tight and difficult to talk. Tears streamed down and when I couldn't speak, I took a deep breath and admitted that this was very hard. I told them that I went upstairs to check on my own daughter, a sixth grader, and how she admitted that she had not really known this teacher. I felt relieved that she was saved from this grief, and also saddened that she never got to know this wonderful person. I told them how lucky we are to have known and loved Mrs. Deichmann. I saw heads nodding and one student said, "knowing nod goes here," which is something she said to them often. I asked what other things she said to them.

What things do you remember about her? What did she teach you? What would make her smile right now? These simple inquiries created a sense of ease in my body, perhaps because I did not have the answers, and also because I knew that they did. They had all kinds of wonderful answers, like hidden gems tucked inside their hearts. As they shared them, very quietly and carefully, the pain I felt in my chest and throat loosened. I felt a new sense of connection, like, "Yes, that was her!" From there, naming the center of immense sorrow, a sense of gratitude connected us. Acknowledging these difficult emotions, and how hard they are to experience, helped us allow their existence as a part of being human. To feel anger, sorrow, and gratitude all at once, like navigating a rowboat across an ocean. We discussed how we can use art to work with difficult emotions and persevere through hard times. Kids paired up or worked individually on their ideas of how to honor their teacher, who, they realized, loved them very much. "There's a difference," I told them, "in having a teacher you really like and having a teacher who truly loves you." Many nodding heads showed me they understood.

These conversations were very difficult, but they all went very well. I think my fear and anticipation of bringing these students into an art studio amidst a tragic loss was strong—I wanted to be honest, to help them feel, to communicate and express honestly, and to support them fully, and not mess it up, or let anyone down. At the same time, I am also heartbroken, in shock, and still devastated myself. "The only way around is through," and I hoped to demonstrate that by example, to help us through this together. This was my very raw, authentic self showing up for my students, and once they understood that, they were able to share from their tender insides too. Now, all my 5th and 7th grade students who knew and loved Mrs. Deichmann are hard at work on creative projects to honor her memory. This would not have been possible without mindfulness practice and authentic connection with my own, inner experience. Finding ways to be present with these difficult and disparate emotions, to see them, accept them, just as they are, like travelers on an overcrowded train, has helped keep us moving forward together.

Julia is undoubtedly surrounded by angels. She is right beside Jesus, she is shining and holy, smiling and making her place in some Godly realm. During the first few days and weeks after she passed, I spoke to her out loud quite often. "Don't worry about your students," I'd tell her. "We've got them. We are here for them, and they are going to be all right. Go be with your family. Say your goodbyes with them." Eventually, when I felt her spirit leave school, I asked her for help. There must be someone you can talk to, Julia- I need a miracle. This was when I was deeply entrenched in the battle of where my mom would go after leaving Highland Hospital. There was immense stress during this time of the pandemic. But I deepened my hope and faith through prayer and meditation.

Jesus healed my shattered heart at the yoga retreat. Mother Mary walked me through the darkest days of being a terrified, single mother. Lord Ganesha could help deliver my mother to a safe refuge much closer to us. Who else can I call on now? Please help, Julia. I trusted Julia to rub elbows with angels just like her. I also repeated the mantra to Ganesha to remove the obstacles in our path, in my mom's path. Om Gam Ganapataye Namaha. Om Gam Ganapataye Namaha. Om Gam Ganapataye Namaha. Om Gam Ganapataye Namaha... I kept the vigil going, like a wind chime in March, like a stream rolling along, as I fell asleep. The mantra became a silent calling from a grateful heart to an old friend. Help us, please. We need a miracle.

Resilience is a buzzword in education now. Thanks to Angela Duckworth's research and her powerful book, Grit. I hope it sticks around a long time. Resilience basically means toughness, and also flexibility—strong *and* flexible. Resilient is what we become when we've survived some difficult stuff in life, persevered, made it through and changed a bit. Circumstances can make us soften in ways that help open our hearts and deepen our compassion to ourselves and others, and life can deepen our resolve, our ability to stick with difficult tasks or rise to meet impossible odds. When we keep moving forward through life, in spite of challenges, we can come out the other side of things more resilient, with a strength that runs deeper.

On a recent visit to see my mom, she told me we were getting a million dollars. "I know you don't believe me, but we are," she said sternly.

"Okay, mom, that's amazing!" I made sure she knew that I was listening, even if I didn't believe it.

"Oh, and I wish you could see the diamonds," she said longingly, looking off in the distance. "I will have to find them to show you," she repeated several times.

Diamonds, I thought, she's seeing diamonds, beautiful, sparkling diamonds that no one else sees. It could be worse. What do diamonds represent anyway? Formed under intense pressure, black coal transforms into a shining diamond. Resilience.

The next week I led a mindfulness lesson on resilience. We took a few deep breaths settling in and defined resilience as toughness that forms after making it through a difficult journey. Getting through this global pandemic, suffering through loss, grief, continuous uncertainty. Advocating for my mom to get into assisted living, out of hospitals and into long-term care was another arduous journey. It reminded me of the diamonds my mom knows are hidden somewhere. She's certain that they're *ours*. These diamonds belong to us. She sees them everywhere now and reaches for them too, only to discover it's a ball of lint, a shiny screw or piece of hardware fixed to her wheelchair.

I tell my students about the journey carbon goes through—extreme pressure and heat, being shot up to the earth's crust through volcanic eruptions, landing under piles of rock and tons of pressure until the carbon is completely transformed. It is no longer black but crystal clear like glass, stronger and tougher, more resilient after its intense journey. The diamonds make me think about all we've been through over the past two years. Surviving the pandemic transformed us through pressure, intense changes, and a long, arduous journey.

"Sometimes we don't feel tough," I said. "Sometimes we feel tender, or sad, we miss someone so much it hurts, or we just feel numb. We can place a hand on our body where we feel we need it and just breathe, knowing that all these difficult emotions are part of living. They are part of the journey."

As we took some deep breaths, sitting with these intense emotions, recognizing all we'd been through, our appreciation for the journey deepened. As we exhaled, we began to realize that we'd made it through. We'd risen, like carbon from the earth's mantle, up through the depths to withstand immense pressures and life-threatening changes. We'd transformed too, and we'd become stronger for it. As we breathed out, we imagined shining from within. We'd become more resilient, and now, we could shine like diamonds. Maybe that's why mom can't find the diamonds. They're inside of us. They're inside all of us who've survived this time and became stronger, clearer, more reflective of the light around us, just like diamonds.

When I wake at five-thirty a.m., it's still dark, the lights of the village twinkling in the valley below. I stretch and move my arms up and down slowly, lifting and lowering with each breath in and out. Sun breaths warm and lift me toward the day, even before the sun rises beyond the great pines. About twenty-five minutes of yoga poses and stretching bring me to a reclined twist and some crunches, helping me find my center and feel ready to greet the day. Dan is by my side doing his own version of a daily self-care routine. Sometimes a thin thread of my most recent dream spills out and I tell him the odd tale. We chuckle or sigh, mention the weather or what may be ahead in our school days. It is a soft start to a fast-paced, demanding day of teaching middle-schoolers. Eventually, coffee and breakfast has me seated facing a wall of windows looking east, watching the sun's magnificent rise. How lucky am I.

Soon after Ada is at the breakfast table too, she mumbles something about a hair in her food. "What, honey? A hair?"

After an eye roll, she repeats, more loudly this time, "No mom, a HERON! I just saw a Heron fly by. There were two, flying that way," she pointed southeast toward Alma Pond. I'm stunned at first but question her to make sure she's identified the bird correctly. "Yes, I'm sure—they have those huge wings and the long legs that stick out the back."

This pair of Great Blue Herons is the first we've seen so far this year, and it's early March, so it's a bit unusual. They may be building nests or scouting out fishing spots, many of which are still icy. Their presence is a signal that spring is unfolding, even when we still feel so tightly wrapped in winter.

For me, it's a reminder that we're cared for, watched over, blessed in so many ways, and ultimately loved by this mysterious, unfathomable, brilliant Universe.

It just never gets old. It feels like your best friend is checking in on you from another world. When we spot a heron, it is a small celebration of being alive in that moment. Another year has passed on Heron hill and these intelligent creatures are somewhere much warmer for the winter season, somewhere they can fish and stay warm high up in their nests. Our garage and my long-awaited yoga studio is nearing completion as we enter another holiday season. Some nights, I feel overwhelmed by the school day, parenting, cooking, cleaning, and the activities of daily living. When I have enough energy, I go up to the studio and sit with Buddha, my beloved teacher, who's moved up and out of the closet. He reminds me to breathe, to settle my body and nervous system a bit, to notice, and breathe. When the days are so short this time of year, I feel sun deprived and weary. This is when I call on spirit guides. When I ask the questions once again. "What should I do now? Which direction should I go? Please give me guidance to move forward through this life. Love is forward…" I sit with Buddha and light candles, shuffling the deck of cards. The first one I chose was a seagull that read, "It is time for deep healing." Surprisingly, after a few days, I began to notice the seagulls. In the parking lots, soaring along the riverbanks and circling over the open areas in the park. "You have wings, for god's sake, what on earth are you doing here? Why don't you fly someplace warm," I think as I watch them. What deep healing do I have left? How do I do it? How do I heal? No one tells you how—not in teaching, and not in life. I think maybe that's because there are infinite possibilities, and you have to keep experimenting with life to find what works best.

Later, sitting in meditation, I placed my right hand on my heart and my left hand on top, sending some loving-kindness into my heart space. Sometimes when I think of my physical heart, it's almost like a strong sack filling and emptying, only there is a residue that clings to the very bottom of the sack. A lot like the water cup I use to clean my paint brushes, or the bucket of sponges in my art classroom. There is always this residue of paint that won't rinse out completely. You gotta scrub it with a brush or a sponge to get it clean. I have to work at it a little for the residue to leave completely. I think my heart is like that. There is some kind of sticky, wounded residue at the very bottom. The seagulls soar overhead reminding me that my heart is something like the deep ocean they know so well. I need to work at cleaning out my heart, because it's as deep as an ocean, with mysterious stuff at the very bottom.

As I sit with my hands over my heart for several evenings after tiring workdays, I finally begin to feel that residue. I simply ask, "what is there that needs healing?" Immediately, I am flooded with thoughts of my mom. The memories come like ocean waves crashing, and ceaseless. Saltwater tears trickle down my face and drip onto my collar bones, pooling in my hands. I feel as though I am being cleansed. Saltwater heals. I realize that the deepest healing I need to do is heal these maternal wounds. I think of her, sending her loving-kindness, wishing her peace, wishing her freedom. When I end my meditation and stand, I feel as though there's a little less residue in the depths of my heart. The water is clean.

The Great Blue Heron

"Make a stand for what you believe in and do what feels right in spite of any disapproval or judgment of others." — Steven D. Farmer's Animal Spirit Cards

Pierre Straub was one of those students who hated high school, and he had plenty of reasons: "It's fucking stupid, I don't care, and I don't want to," were just a few of them. From a teacher's perspective, though, he was up against a lot. Living in a rural place with a single parent who walks to their job as a gas station attendant, no form of transportation, and very little income left Pierre lacking resources and support as he navigated those very complex pubescent years. On top of that, the rules and total lack of choice and freedom in public high school are stifling for most teens. As an art teacher, I assigned very little homework, but with drawing, it's all about *practice*. Contrary to popular belief, drawing is not a talent you're born with, or some natural gift humans do masterfully after emerging from the womb. Everyone can draw, yes, it's called mark-making. We do this naturally as children. If you want to develop what might be a natural affinity to drawing, painting, or other creative ventures, experimentation and practice are needed to develop these into skills. Motivation, inspiration, patience, and a splash of creativity all help grow those skills even further, with practice. Becoming good at drawing is like becoming good at basketball or ice-skating— you visualize, train, and practice. Creating comes from hard work and dedication.

I gave one sketchbook assignment a week, and students could choose from a list of suggestions or do their own, due every Monday. Pierre never completed his assignments, but I could see his ability in class and made sure he passed the class based on his participation and attendance. His sour attitude made it challenging to assign these grades at times, so I would refer back to the many reasons life sucked for him, folding in some grace. Occasionally, I gave him a "come to Jesus talk," parenting the best way I knew how, from a place of honesty and love. I knew he could do anything he wanted if he set his mind to it and became determined to practice and develop his skills.

Eventually, Pierre graduated, found some local roofing and flooring jobs, and soon learned just how difficult it was to earn enough money to pay for a car. He was learning a lot about life and returned to school for some help in the guidance office during the next year. He was becoming deter-mined to forge his own path, and he wanted it to be a creative one. Once he found the art of tattooing, his determination took root. He applied patience, practice, and inspiration to his newly found craft and spent many years developing his skills as a tattoo artist. He practiced, not because it was assigned to him, but because he truly wanted to. I stayed in touch with Pierre via social media and cheered him on from a distance. I told him how proud I was of him, for finding what he loved to do and for not giving up.

Throughout this pandemic, I've been tested, as a parent, as a teacher, an artist, and as a woman. There is so much I'd like to adjust about the world—to inject a deep love and compassion into our modern society, to create equity in the workplace, politics, and the judicial system. When I grasp at making everything better, *better than normal,* I find myself angry and frustrated and once again return to my knees, talking to God, asking questions. During the darkest times of my life, I asked if anyone else knew what was in my heart, if I was completely alone in the world, and if anyone out there cared for me, loved me in a way that was deeper and stronger than all the human relations I'd known. Each time I reached out from these vulnerable places in my heart, I was given a gift. I learned from that film, What the Bleep Do We Know, to ask for a sign that I would know and have no doubt about when I saw it. "Please show me you're there, that you care for me, that I am not alone, that you are indeed guiding me along this path, and please, make it something I will know for sure, beyond the shadow of any doubt, that this is coming from you." I spent many nights on my knees, salty tears streaming down like waterfalls, begging, and pleading for help from the Universe, from Mother Nature, from God, or whoever could hear the voice inside my heart. Each time, soon after, I would see a Great Blue Heron.

The first time, while driving to the grocery store, I crossed a bridge spanning a swamp, turned my head and made eye contact with a heron standing in the water. That piercing bird stare prompted a slow-motion pass over a bridge I will never forget. Another time, looking up, there was a Great Blue Heron flying directly overhead as I drove along a usual route. It began to feel like I had a grand, feathered chaperone. They are unmistakable birds with enormous wingspans and long legs that stretch flat out behind them in flight. When you see one, you know it. Other instances, these magnificent birds became bookmarks in my daily life, seen on a tapestry, a deck of cards, in a magazine while waiting in a dental office, or even, in a song title on the radio. In this very consistent way, I learned that the Great Blue Heron was my answer from the Universe. In some native American traditions, this would be a revered spirit animal. Herons represent balance, self-determination, and self-reliance. They were my guides, showing me that I knew what was in my heart better than anyone else, and to trust it; to stand up for what I believed was right for me and keep moving forward.

Herons migrate for thousands of miles every year to build nests, give birth and raise their young. As cold weather emerges in the fall, they begin flying south again to enjoy better fishing and warmer nights. They know the way without GPS, AAA, or Expedia, they trust their internal knowledge and go. It works every time. When Dan and I decided to buy our plot of land in the village of Wellsville, we would walk up to scout out the overgrown pastureland, make trails and begin hacking away the buckthorn and bull thistle, attempting to visualize a long driveway and where the house could be. During spring and summer months, there were plenty of jobs to do preparing the land for a house. We would walk Henry up to Pine Street to explore and begin shaping the land anew. Almost every time we visited; we saw herons.

They would fly overhead from their nesting grounds, which we discovered nearby, deep into a wooded area west of Highland Avenue. They build magnificent nests near the top of tall red pines. The herons co-parent in these nests, taking turns fishing at Alma Pond or in the Genesee River. Often, they "tag-team," leaving one adult at home in the nest while the other goes to work. We'd spot one heading home to the rookery and soon after, another great-winged bird would fly from nest to water, as they took turns fishing and residing in the treetops. Herons are superb co-parents. These magnificent birds have become role models as well as trusted spirit guides, continuously showing me a steady way of attending to life as it unfolds. Because our new home was being built directly beneath the commuter path of the local herons, we began referring to our home here as Heron Hill. Recalling that first sighting over the bridge so many years ago, when I knew beyond the shadow of a doubt, that someone, somewhere loved my heart and cared for my dreams, and watched over my life, putting down roots here seemed like good magic. I could not have devised a better plan on my own. This was far better than I could have ever imagined; this had grace folded in.

After attending too many funerals, supporting friends, family, and students through one crisis after another, after suffering through the "milder" Omicron version of Covid-19 in 2021 even while triple-vaccinated, I became so weary. So very tired of the uncertainty, of canceling plans or refusing to make any, skipping every and all form of social festivity, these past few years have aged me tenfold. I was ready for some change. A haircut and a massage were a good start as these things became feasible once again. The next step, as my new Art & Yoga studio is being built over the new garage, was a tattoo. And I knew just the artist.

Pierre drew a Great Blue Heron and koi fish swirling around its long, stick legs from just below my left shoulder, to a hands-width beyond my elbow. Nicely hidden, only for whom I choose to share it. Pierre and I talked for the six hours he drew. He was thirty-two with ten years of tattoo-ing experience. He drew with inspiration, determination, skill, and patience, using needles dipped into permanent ink, into my flesh. "I can't believe you're basically getting a sleeve for your first tattoo," he commented as he worked.

I trusted him fully and said so. I knew what was in my heart, because it propelled me along a journey with graceful guides and to a loving partner, only to settle beneath a blessed path in the sky. Each time I see a Great Blue Heron, I take a deep breath, and say, "Thank you for teaching me to trust what's inside, thank you for seeing me here, for loving me like you do."

The start of the next school year brought some surprises. My dear friend, Rhiannon, whom I taught with for the past twelve years, resigned. I would need to support her decision as a friend as well as help find and interview a new art teacher to take her place at Genesee Valley. Soon, we hired a former student, Cassidy, who had been a shining light in high school and sometimes stayed after to paint with Ada when she was in first or second grade. With Cassidy still in college and completing her bachelor's degree, I would gladly be her mentor. Although this meant more hours of work, I never hesitated. I was already committed to sharing the job of middle school student council with our guidance counselor and hoping to incorporate mindfulness lessons into a wider range of classes. My plate was filling fast as the school year closed in. I got a phone call about a week before we were to report back to school for professional development days before students returned. "Your schedule has changed," my principal, Sara, said flatly, "and you will be teaching Jag Design with Kim." I was surprised that this was coming as an order rather than an option or possibility. It was already done and on my schedule.

"I didn't want to do that, Sara," was all I could get out. I said nothing of my plate being full already, of taking on more responsibility, or Ada wanting to play volleyball and track, and the hours needed to parent my child. I did not want to teach this course, not because it wasn't great or because I disliked the other co-teacher, but because it was not the path I wanted to take. I squeezed the heron tattooed on my arm and took a deep breath. I will not be doing that. I have to stand up for what I want and speak honestly whenever I need to.

Heron Hill Yoga has been built. Nearly ready for visitors and students, things are coming together. There were days, living with Chad, when I would immediately cry upon waking. My truest, most trusted escape from living a life I felt trapped in, a life that conflicted with what I knew in my heart, was sleep. Sleep was sweet relief, and upon waking, I would sob realizing I was still trapped, still slogging through the muck of my life. There were long, dark nights of the soul, vicious arguments, terrible storms, and loss. Now when I sleep, I often dream about Dan who is asleep beside me. One morning I woke from a wonderful dream where I was peacefully resting in Dan's arms. He has a way of wrapping himself around me, so that I feel safe and cherished. In his embrace I feel like a child who is valued, loved, and protected. I woke up in Dan's embrace and felt a wave of joy roll through my body, just like the hummingbird vibrations I experienced in the sweat lodge ceremony. I woke up from a beautiful dream that made me feel cherished to a life that was a mirror of that dream. A life centered on Love. A life with a man that I dream about and still do today. I'd found a partner who shows his love instead of just saying it. Remembering the dreams deep inside me, reminding myself of my dearest wishes, to live a life centered in love, led me to a life I love. With a lot of guidance, support from family and friends, and I believe, some divine intervention, I've found myself at home on Heron Hill.

A drum circle with a group of like-minded friends welcoming the full moon was a wonderful way to create some good energy in the yoga studio. One step at a time, finding balance between work and life, self-care and teaching, fun, play, rest and sleep is a dynamic endeavor I'm doing better with, although there is a fine line that seems delicate and easy to cross. There's so much I long to do, to make, to create, to learn, to understand, to share, to celebrate, and a small sliver of the day that's left for it all. Resting my attention on this screen is one way to create, to be present. The first official yoga class I led at Heron Hill Yoga was about Self-Care, and it was a rough lesson to learn preparing for the class.

Two trips to urgent care and a strong antibiotic later, I am free from pain yet still have fluid in my left ear. I found the work of a trusted energy healer to be invaluable and am going to continue seeking out her services. There seems to be so much change taking place just below the surface—in the earth, and within me, possibly within us all. I'm not sure where it will lead us, but I hope it will be toward healing and positive change. Another doctor visit left me with drugs I don't trust and don't want to take. I look at the orange pill bottle and my childhood co-dependence rushes to the surface. My mom's plastic shopping bags filled with prescription pills. "If you don't have one of these, you can take this instead," she'd say. Or, in a red-faced rage, her blood pressure rising, "I need to take my medication!" she'd shout, shaking and angry. I look at the orange pill bottle and toss it into a cabinet. Instead, I take some deep breaths and watch some videos about all-natural healing and lymphatic drainage. Eventually, what works to clear my sinusitis and double ear infections is mullein oil with a few drops of tea tree oil dripped directly into each ear. After months of suffering and reaching out to for-profit health-care systems for help, I receive healing free from YouTube. Lesson learned: I am in charge of my health, wellness, and healing. I can choose who I trust and how to care for my body.

The next gift on this healing journey is a sprained ankle. Thrilled to be outdoors again, feeling relieved and ready for some physical labor, I grab our electric string trimmer and trot down our gravel drive. The blue sky pulls my attention upward and I send out a message of thanks. Next, I step into a hole disguised by tall grass and roll my ankle violently out of control, hear a crack, like a branch snapping, and fall to the ground. Instant, intense pain rushes through and up my right leg. I lay there in the soft grass, step my foot onto a cloud above and breathe. Holding my ankle, the pain intensifies. Wondering if it's broken, I hold still and watch the sky. Just then, a great blue heron flies overhead, but instead of flying in its usual straight path to and from the nest, it circles overhead, as if to say, "I see you down there all broken."

"Okay, I say, I will trust whatever lies ahead. I'm listening." I lay there and held my growing ankle joint and called Dan. "I think I broke my ankle," I told him. Dan came running down the rough and rocky slope to kneel beside me. He stroked my hair and talked to me, which was surprisingly helpful. I kept my foot up in the blue sky as I wiped away a few tears and eventually got up and limped away to finish what I started, which was to trim the tall grass by the mailbox and roadside.

Later I realized that was foolish and it was time to go to urgent care, which closed early, forcing me to hobble further through the hospital to the ER. Several medical personnel checked up on me once, but only the receptionist checked in multiple times during my two-and-a-half-hour visit. X-rays showed no break or fissure, so "It's just a bad sprain," was my parting gift as I limped toward the exit. The bubbly receptionist brought me a wheelchair and pushed me out to Dan in the idling car. I squeezed the heron tattoo on my left arm after buckling up and realized that I cannot properly stand like the heron does with such stability and grace. Life is a constant stream of change, and I'm being asked to change my daily life in a radical way, for now, to allow healing to begin. Maybe tree pose, dancing crane, or heron pose is what I'm meant to focus on, but not for a while. I have new work to do. The work of elevating my feet, icing a swollen joint, and resting—some of the most challenging things I've had to do is non-doing: rest, stillness, and patience.

Love is Forward

"I am not what happened to me. I am what I choose to become." — Carl Jung

"Love changes us and helps us move forward in life. It often helps us become the people we've always wanted to be and move away from the people we were. Love transforms us in the best of ways, allowing us only to look back on a memory of our former self." — Adam Wilde

O ver two decades ago, I lived alone in a small, one-bedroom house in Alfred, New York. My elderly landlord named Lois lived next door, and she referred to my little rental cottage as "the chateau." Lois was about ninety then and very intelligent, a quaker, and lived a privileged, yet simple life. She went out every day for a walk, and despite her macular degeneration, she got around on her own just fine. She loved the little chateau and told stories about how Bill Underhill, the famous art professor at AU lived there, and later his daughter took it over and used it as an art studio. It had a fireplace as well as electric heat, a very small bathroom and a tiny loft balcony above the family room that felt unsafe to stand up in. The one bedroom above the kitchen had gabled ceilings and I couldn't stand up straight in the room without hitting my head. My futon bed took up most of the painted wood floor, and I cherished my own little nest, despite its shortcomings. Often, the sorority across the street had parties or strange rushing requirements where a slew of college girls went out into the street to sing at the top of their lungs. These occasions woke me in the early morning hours, but I often fell back to sleep before I had to wake at five-thirty a.m. to get ready for my teaching job. It was this waking and drifting back into sleep before waking again that often led to vivid dreams during the golden hour.

It had only been a few months since I'd found myself frozen, mid-stride, staring down the barrel of a handgun on my lunch break in Rochester. One morning, while I was waking in the cozy loft of the Alfred chateau, but not awake, I was sitting at the feet of God (or someone who was the Source of all Life, *of my life*), and I became filled with an understanding of the infinite love a parent has for their child. I suddenly understood how much God loves all of us, all of creation, all life. This force, or Higher Power, emanated joy and boundless love. A voice spoke in my mind that said, "Love is forward," and I woke up with a feeling of listening to someone who had just been speaking to me. "Love is forward," I repeated to myself as I woke, and I've never forgotten that dream, that morning waking in the little chateau, full of wonder and awe, experiencing a sense of complete bliss. This may have been a brief glimpse of enlightenment. After I became fully conscious, however, the feeling I had, the experience I had, faded into a memory. I had no idea what it meant, "Love is forward," but I felt wonderful, like I was completely at ease, knowing how loved I was, and filled with hope and a renewed willingness to keep living, to keep moving forward.

Soon after that, I met Chad Rafferty and my life changed forever. Perhaps that dream was a parting gift before embarking on the terrible, soul-crushing journey that was the twelve-year relationship with a recovering alcoholic. I'm glad I still have that memory, right down to the overwhelming, indescribable feeling of awe and unconditional love that included me, encompassed me, and possibly, protected me through it all.

Toward the end of our marriage, I would often wake up next to Chad and immediately begin crying, a sense of dread and disillusionment would sweep over me immediately upon waking. I used sleep as a refuge to escape my reality during this time in my life. I couldn't see a way of leaving without hurting Ada like I'd been hurt as a child her age. I couldn't see a way around that, so I felt stuck, trapped in a relationship I'd outgrown. I tried to explain the feeling by telling Chad and our therapist that our marriage was like putting on shoes that I loved but had become too tight and painful. I just didn't fit into our relationship anymore. He would call me selfish and crazy. "So, you're going to be happy while the rest of us will be miserable, and that's not fair," he'd persist, tightening the snare. Eventually, I stopped believing those thoughts and found the courage to insist, "We can *all* be happy."

For the first few years of my new life with Dan, I would dream about sleeping next to him. Dan had a way of wrapping me up with his arms and legs, big spoon style, making me feel cherished and protected. "Are you comfortable? Do you need anything?" he'd check before he allowed himself to drift off to sleep. I would fall asleep, perfectly content, feeling safe, loved, and even treasured. We both gave each other a sense of gratitude that we'd found each other later in life.

I would dream about my reality and wake to that same reality, realizing I'd found the man of my dreams, that I was actually living my dream. I'd found a way out of the trap by insisting on real love and by creating this new reality. Every morning still, when my mind slowly becomes active again, moving out of the dream state and back into consciousness, I say, "Thank you, thank you, thank you." I talk to the Higher Power I felt that morning in my little chateau many years ago, because I know that I'm heard and loved. I also understand now that I am co-creating my experience.

I'm Sorry. Please Forgive Me. Thank You. I Love You.

"Story, as it turns out, was crucial to our evolution-more so than opposable thumbs. Opposable thumbs let us hang on; story told us what to hang on to." — Lisa Cron

"There is no greater agony than bearing an untold story inside you." — Maya Angelou

I was abused as a child. Not sexually, but sometimes physically. Sometimes physically by my mom. A lack of genuine hugs and generally rough treatment seems more like neglect, but when peppered with slaps, irate screaming, swearing, and sudden attacks made it lean closer to abuse. Her addictions and mental health helped shape me into a co-dependent for many decades. My older brother abused me physically for a period of about three years. Today I know that's called sibling abuse, but I didn't know it then. He often wanted to wrestle with me. He must have been into the WWF in the 1980s, because he always wanted to smear my face into a carpet, the grass, or the folded down backseat of our brown, Chevy Chevette. Three years older and twice my size, he once knocked one of my teeth out while we were "rough-housing," as my mom called it. If it got too rough and I began to scream or cry, he would mock me, and my mother sighed or screamed but never intervened. One of the scariest things he ever did to me was trap me in a sleeping bag until I couldn't breathe. I begged and pleaded for him to let me out, because I truly thought I was going to die. When George Floyd begged for his life from Minneapolis police officers, his "I can't breathe" plea was familiar to me. What more are you supposed to say? Unlike those officers, my brother found a shred of decency, some spark of empathy inside and let me out just in time. Every time I survived an interaction with Freddy, I hated him a little more. I didn't know it was wrong for my mom to allow such treatment or to scream at us to shut up and slam her bedroom door, ignoring any obligation to teach us how to resolve our conflicts, or how to simply co-exist. I believe the pain Freddy felt from losing our dad got expressed just a bit every time he punched me for taking the remote or for just being the annoying little sister. Eventually Freddy became too busy with friends and chasing girls to bother with me, and I saw him less and less. I know now that my Adverse Child Experiences (ACE score) was rather high from what I'd experienced growing up. I survived it all, though, and promised myself that one day, I would be nothing like them. I would be *happy*.

My mom struggled with parenting, was a stressed-out, single parent doing the best she could. I forgive her now for not protecting me like I needed. My dad was not a big part of our lives. It was like having an absent father who was right there. Even though we saw him every other weekend, and he lived only twenty minutes away, he was forced to choose between his kids and his new wife, and he chose her. Karen. She made rules that seemed impossible to master as a kid, like "you are never to mention your mother in our house. You cannot call her on our phone or say her name or talk about her at all."

I later learned that things like this, along with being told I was not wanted, is called emotional child abuse. My brother and I were used to lending a hand on the farm and washed all the dishes by hand after every meal. Oddly enough, those times were peaceful between my brother and I, we were so busy completing chores together. Our mutual disappointment created a bond between us on those weekend visits. We were sent to rooms called "the blue room," and "the rose room," which had electricity but no heat.

I still remember that the blue room had a beautiful art deco painting of Jesus hanging over the bed in an oval frame. It was a white-skinned, blue-eyed Jesus, which I knew could not have been right historically and geographically speaking, but he looked like he cared about you. Of course, my brother had the blue room, and I wondered if he ever talked to Jesus on the wall. I know I would have.

Some of Karen's rules were:

1. Never mention your mom out loud in their house, ever.
2. Never let any of the cats out of the house (even if they pushed past you like a rocket every time you opened the door).
3. Always wait until everyone's at the table before eating, and drink all your milk (even if it makes you sick and you hate it).
4. Eat everything on your plate, no exceptions.
5. Ask to be excused from the table.

6. Pick up your chair when you push it away from the table, so you don't scratch the wood floor and ruin it.

7. Wash, rinse, and dry all the dishes by hand and leave them on the counter.

8. Do not pick any flowers from the property intending to bring them home to your mother, because that would violate Rule #1, even if it was unspoken.

9. Always keep your shoes or boots on when inside the house (even though the rest of your week you were required to remove your shoes upon entering your other parent's ever-changing apartment house).

10. Go to church and sing all the words as written in the hymnal, with vim and vigor!

11. Judge and scoff at anyone with democratic or liberal views.

12. No second chances: Anyone who threatens your lifestyle shall be judged harshly without forgiveness.

I'm sure there were more, but those were the biggies. Of course, we violated all the rules at some point, which is what gave life to a new rule. Also, as soon as she and my dad arrived anywhere to visit—my graduation, a family picnic, or any special event—she discussed the best way to get home and precisely what time they would be leaving. They had to get back to the dogs. When I was a kid, it was her dog Lady, then Bess and Chester, the red-boned coon hound. Today it's Penny and Reggie, two anti-social rescues.

Their local newspaper decided to run a story on the anniversary of the discovery of the Bloomfield mastodon, and Karen made sure they included that she and my dad had no children, that their beloved dogs were their children. She gave me a copy of it to keep in case maybe I forgot that my dad chose her instead of us. My dad became a local celebrity for unearthing the mastodon skeleton, speaking at Rotary and Lions Clubs about his adventure digging up the bones and all he'd learned about it.

My version was different. It involved a newly discovered father-daughter relationship not everyone was comfortable reading about. But I submitted it and made copies anyway. I was given an honorable mention for the graduating thesis competition, and the dean put an award around my neck when I crossed the stage at graduation. Unfortunately, I never enjoyed this success because I was too worried about navigating my parents who refused to speak to each other or occupy the same room.

My mom was seated on one side of the giant, white carrier dome, and my dad and Karen were on the other. There were roughly 40,000 people in between. I was expected to navigate the crowd to greet the opposing players, make peace and share detailed plans. Continuing to live with surreal rules that catered to the comfort of a few people in charge felt weary and unacceptable at that point. I was exhausted by it all.

About a year later, another surprise came when Karen invited me over for lunch. I was glad to see them and we sat outside on the porch after we ate. Karen pulled out a six page, hand-written letter and read it aloud to me. She admitted that all her rules and treatment of us kids growing up was unkind, unacceptable even. She was apologizing! I was stunned and didn't know what to say, where to begin. "I forgive you," I said, when she finished reading, because that seemed like the only response that could meet the courage I'd just witnessed. They began smiling and laughing lightly, clearly relieved. Karen and I clasped hands and began to talk for real for the first time in my life. My dad looked just as happy.

My father, Jay Buchholz, is a man of values, kindness, education, and interest. He came from a small house with four other siblings in the tiny town of Whitesville, New York. He went to Alfred State college after returning from four years in the Air Force, worked hard, and got everything he wanted. He scrimped and saved and retired a millionaire at age fifty-one. He worked for Eastman Kodak in Rochester, like lots of our parents did back in the '80s in Rochester. My dad hired and fired people for the HR department, and they offered him an early retirement deal he couldn't refuse. He became a master gardener and worked in his garden, hunted, did Karen's bidding, which involved most of the cooking and cleaning, and continues to do so happily today at eighty years-old.

My dad is a storyteller. He loved talking about the Bloomfield Mastodon. He gladly recalls his childhood in Whitesville. "We were always chasing some kind of animal," he said about his siblings on the farm. "There was always a cow, pig or some other animal that got loose that we had to herd back into the barn."

This Buchholz family of seven shared a tiny farmhouse with one bathroom and housed all five children upstairs in an attic space you could not stand in upright unless you were close to the stairs. My grandfather was a strict, hard-working German man. "I remember having to help my dad on the tractor way up on the hill when it was time for my baseball game to start. He wouldn't let me go until the work was done, and I could hear them playing the national anthem. I wanted to get that work done as fast as possible, and I did too. As soon as he said so, I ran as fast as I could to the school to get in the game." My dad's relationship with his dad revolved around work. My relationship with my dad revolved around memory and story. For many years growing up, I cried myself to sleep missing my dad. I must have been sixteen before I realized that it was never going to be like it was when I was little. Somehow, I had to let go.

My dad's been retired for thirty years. He rarely calls, we see each other once or twice a year and have a very limited relationship. I talk more freely with co-workers and post-office employees, to be honest. If he were a cad, this might be acceptable. What's tough about our distance is that he's a wonderful person. One beautiful thing that came from the extreme political positions of this pandemic era was that my brother and dad connected over their love for Trump and conservatism.

"Dad said that he really admired us for not getting vaccinated," my brother boasted about how he and his wife get together with Dad and Karen on occasion.

"That's great," I replied. "You all deserve each other," I thought as I recalled my mom using the same phrase when hearing about Karen's maltreatment of us after a weekend visit. "Ugh, they deserve each other," she'd say with a hint of disgust in her voice. There was also a smidge of acceptance, which is also what I felt, perhaps a letting go.

Somehow, my mom parented us for the both of them. My dad bailed on his responsibility of being a parent; of knowing, guiding, loving and being part of his children's lives. My mom just did it all on her own. Some of the most wonderful times I've spent with my mom have been right inside the nursing home walls, or in its courtyard on sunny days, just looking up at the sky or noticing the birds or changes in the plants and trees, just being together. The Parkinson's erased any need to be right, to control or to agree and simplified every visit into time spent together. My mom told me during my last few visits that she was ready to go. I was relieved in a way, but I realized that she meant she was ready to move again—to move into a little house in Alfred and ride her bike around town. One Sunday afternoon I found most of her clothes spread out all over her bed, as though she'd been emptying drawers and packing her things. "I was out in the rain packing my car in the middle of the night, and they came out and got me and brought me back in," she told me. She hadn't had a car in years, and I knew this was another fantasy, but maybe it was more than that. Maybe it was her preparing to leave. I tried not to notice her roommate Lucy (who also had Parkinson's) as she occupied her silent, frozen body being fed by Elderwood staff. I prayed my mom would be spared that horror, being trapped inside a body that was being kept alive long after her use of it had gone.

With all this, I was still unprepared for the phone call on Saturday morning. I was awake around 5:30 that morning but didn't want to get up. I watched the light in our bedroom change and noticed a strange feeling of resistance in me that

I couldn't quite place, like a weighted blanket pressing on my chest. I instantly thought of her and spoke out loud, "Mom." I wanted to stay in bed all day but didn't know why. Reluctantly, I pulled myself out of bed to notice a missed call from Elderwood at five thirty-nine a.m.

I called and had to leave a message. When a nurse called back, she said, "I don't know how to tell you this, but your mom passed away this morning. She asked for a drink of water, and after she took a sip, she slumped over and was gone. I'm so sorry." I took a deep breath and thanked her. Just as I ended the call an uncontrolled sobbing escaped from my body as my torso shook in waves. Ada and Dan ran to me and wrapped their arms around me. Ada kissed my head several times, and I simultaneously felt held together and utterly wrecked. As my crying subsided, they loosened their circle around me. It was over. She was gone. "She was ready to go," I told them, but I wasn't there for her. "I should have been there," I muttered, everything about me sloppy and wet.

Within an hour I was sitting next to my mother's corpse. Her head tilted upward, mouth agape. I lifted her hands and immediately felt the stiffness of her body. Her body was now an empty vessel like I'd never known before. She was no longer in there, my mom. Mama. Oh, *mom…*

I cleaned her forehead, hands, and then feet with a cool washcloth, showing my love and saying goodbye. "Thank you for being my mom," I whispered, as Dan packed up her clothes and what little remained in her small space. I swiped lavender essential oil across her forehead and rubbed her stiffened hands with lotion, understanding that this would be the last time I would ever get to do such a thing. It was not that she was leaving, and I had to prepare for that, but that she was already gone. She was ready to move again, and this was her only way out. Later it dawned on me that somehow, she knew this and that she may have died prematurely because we placed her in the nursing home. "I'm locked up in here," she'd say. Yet she escaped without help from anyone. She was ready to go, and she left.

I soon realized that the weight I felt that morning my mom passed was my mom leaving this world. She was hugging me goodbye. For about two weeks I wrestled with guilt, moving into grief like a thick swamp, mucked up to my waist. The sacred Hawaiian practice called Ho'oponopono helped me through the Grief Swamp one day at a time. Often, just being conscious was exhausting. Feeling everything and accepting it was exhausting, much like after the death of my marriage. This practice had led me through grief then, why not now?

Settling into a comfortable seat, or just collapsing into bed, I would call out to my mom. This was usually silent, but I could feel my heart crying out, the vibrations from deep sadness were pulsing out of me, into the world. I'm sorry. "I'm so sorry, mom, I'm sorry you had this terrible disease. I'm sorry we put you in the nursing home. **I'm sorry.** I'm sorry. I'm so sorry, mom. Eventually, finding my breath, allowing the tears to slow, I was ready for the next line. **Please forgive me.** I know you already do, but I have to ask, and I have to apologize to release all this sorrow. Please, forgive me. **Thank you.** Thank you for forgiving me. Thank you for being my mom. Thank you for all you taught me. Thank you. Thank you for the time we spent together. **I love you.** I love you so deeply, in spite of all your mistakes and mine. I love you like I never knew when you were still here for me to tell you. I love you. I love you. I love you.

Several days following my mom's death felt very heavy, as if I was carrying Dan's giant, Army-issue duffel bag on my back all day long. Ho'oponopono was my guide through the Grief Swamp each day spread before me to trudge through. After a week or so, I was able to sit with the meditation and move through it more cleanly. "Mom, I'm so sorry. Please forgive me. Thank you. I love you." Sitting with the weight of what I was feeling slowly became easier. I reminded myself that there is no death. There is *life* after life. There is another dimension where we go home to Oneness, where somehow, we are embraced by our beloved Creator. We are safe, and all is well. I remember to trust this belief. I remember the film I love: Everything, Everywhere, All at Once, and think of the hot-dog finger dimension and giggle. I want to believe that they got it right in that movie. There is life, after life, after life, after life, yet it's all happening, somehow, simultaneously, right now. When you meditate, you can tap into your highest self and transcend all dimensions. "Let me know when you get there, mom, but make sure it's a sign I will recognize and know, without any doubt, that it's from you, letting me know you're Home, safe and sound."

She told me several times that she chased after a rainbow once. I'm ashamed to admit this, but I thought, "What an idiot!" What I actually said was more like, "Mom, that's absurd. It's made of light and will always look like it's moving." She clucked out some laughter and said, "Well, I know that now, but back then, I really wanted to find the end and get the pot of gold."

Rainbows are a big deal. I've had arguments about rainbows, dressed up as the natural phenomena for Halloween, and pulled over while driving on several occasions to witness the spontaneous beauty of a rainbow stretching across the sky. They're not truly bow-shaped, but full circles. I discovered this accidentally when I left a candle burning in the bathroom while I showered. The steamy glass door provided the moisture needed for the candlelight to pass through, and bam! There was a rainbow circling the candle's flame. A full-circle rainbow. Two weeks after my mom left the nursing home on her own accord, we had intense rainbow weather. Mountainous cumulus clouds piled high with small breaks of blue to let sunbeams through. "This is rainbow weather," I thought to myself. I went outside to watch the sky as rain showers slowed. I sat on the picnic table and noticed extremely odd, mountainous clouds that seemed to be building upward, like a tower. When I looked around, I discovered a rainbow weaving in and out of these unusual clouds. As my gaze slowly traversed its colors, and my head tilted up, a hummingbird hovered directly above me. I gasped and immediately thought of my mom sitting on the front porch at the farm, hummingbird feeders overhead, swaying in the wind, hummingbirds darting in and out, around obstacles like kids in a playground. In a moment, it was gone, faster than a drone, and I asked, "Mom, you're home?" As I studied the sky again, I noticed a second rainbow beneath the first: a smaller, fainter rainbow but growing stronger, its color slowly gaining intensity. One for her, and one for me. She'd found the end of the rainbow, or perhaps, she's discovered, as I have, that there is no end.

Where had she been for the past two weeks? Was she completing a Life-Review? Sitting on a cloud somewhere? Haunting her childhood bedroom? Muddling her way through some other dimension? Or maybe, it wasn't two full weeks, but just a moment, or a brief, interstellar journey through time and space. Who's she with? *Her parents.* She's with her mom and dad. She called them mama and daddy, and she said mama with fear and daddy with sweetness, every time.

Later the next day, as I held this question in my heart, "Who's she with now?" a Taylor Swift song came on the radio I'd never heard before, called Betty. My mom's older sister's name was Betty, and they were close. Aunt Betty passed away several years ago, and we visited her quite a bit before she moved on. She was one of the sweetest, most loving, most generous people I've ever known. While listening to Taylor sing, "…I'm only seventeen, I don't know anything, but I know I miss you…" I realized this: my mom was with her sister Betty. I didn't need to worry anymore, she was home safe, with her parents, with her sister, with Oneness, our beloved Maker of Life and Rainbows. I started to remember to breathe again, deeper inhales, longer, slower exhales. I didn't even have to let go anymore, I just needed to accept that she was now in good company, in a lovelier place, in a whole new dimension.

Before all this peace and acceptance I had to figure out how to write an obituary everyone she ever knew would read.

I had to plan a funeral and make decisions nonstop for an entire, eternal week. We had to get to the funeral home in Homer, New York on time, ready to greet everyone she knew that was still alive. I had to face Evan, her boyfriend she left on the farm. When I saw him, he said, "I never, in a million years, thought that anything like this would ever happen." I was stunned into silence until I could only utter, "Really?" When it was my turn behind the podium, however, I was prepared.

After Reverend Alan read bible passages and spoke about my mom in such a warm, loving way, "Pat had a gift for moving," he quipped, he invited me to come to the podium and share my own witness of her life. Shaking, and tearful, I composed myself slowly, standing in front of the crowded room. I asked everyone to bear with me, and took a deep breath:

My mom was a difficult woman. She said things like, "You're wearing that?" and "Do as I say, not as I do." As Karen Karbo writes, "a difficult woman…is a person who believes her needs, passions, and goals are at least as important as those of everyone around her." My mom worked so hard to take care of us kids and she laughed as easily as she screamed. My brother and I visited our grandparents here in Homer quite a lot growing up. Meadow Drive is a sacred place to me. My mom's mother was loving but strict. I thought that removing your shoes when entering the house was Japanese, but it also came from Eloise Wall, and her home was spic and span, all the time.

One of my mom's favorite phrases was always, "don't look a gift horse in the mouth," as we rolled our eyes at the orange in the toe of the Christmas stocking, or underwear as a gift for any occasion. She explained the phrase a few times, for added effect. "If someone gives you a horse, you can bet it's a pretty old one, and so you'd look at its teeth to see just how old that horse might be. Instead, just be grateful someone's giving you anything at all!" she'd say, shaking her finger at me.

I was grateful. I was aware that she'd made a big sacrifice, going back to school as a single parent, being paid far less than her worth and far less than most men in business. I could see she was stressed most of the time. She suffered from migraines, allergies, hypertension, and other ailments caused by our stressful, modern lifestyle. She'd come home after six p.m. exhausted and make us dinner. Quite often, the Masciangelos fed me and surrounded me with love, so my mom could relax. For this extended family I was, and still am, very grateful. My mom's struggle taught me about the importance of self-care and stress management. If it wasn't for her struggle, I may not have become as interested in yoga and meditation, which is what helps me find balance and peace in my life today.

Another Grandma Pat phrase was, "People in glass houses should not throw stones." She said it was translated from Chinese, and I'm not sure, but I think she may have gotten it from a fortune cookie. It holds true either way, though. We are all living in "glass houses," aren't we? Some of us are in glass castles, some are in glass bubbles or boxes, but we are all living in delicate, vulnerable environments that can be cracked and damaged by others. The harder we are on each other, the more damaged and hurt we feel. If we remember to lift each other up, invite each other over for dinner some-times, refrain from judgments and criticism, we might all feel safer and more able to relax. My mom showed me (with a smile, or hello, or just holding a door for someone) that a little kindness goes a long way. She may have been difficult, but she was also kind. And as Ram Das said, "We are all walking each other home." I hope she has a speedy and safe journey home. We love you, mom.

Now, I'd like to lead a brief meditation on Loving-kind-ness, and if you'd like to follow along, all you have to do is repeat the phrases, out loud or silently to yourself, whichever you choose. If you don't want to participate, that's okay too, just ignore me. So, let's sit nice and tall and take a deep breath. You may want to clasp your hands or place them on your legs…Now, let's take the deepest breath we've had all day, as you exhale relaxing the shoulders down the back. Just notic-ing the natural flow of breath for a moment…love and kind-ness starts with meeting your own needs, and believing your needs and passions are equally important—so just repeating:

"May I be safe, May I be happy, May I be free, May I live in peace."

Take a deep breath and notice how those words feel as they sink in.

And for Pat, or anyone else you'd like to send this out to, "May you be safe, May you be happy, May you be free, May you go in peace."

Take another deep breath and notice how it feels to give some loving-kindness away. Now think of someone in your life that is a difficult person, for whatever reason. Picture their face and imagine their voice…this person is also in a glass house, in need of some kindness…send this next one out to them: "May you be safe, May you be happy, May you be free, May you live in peace."

Notice how different that might feel for you. And finally, let's expand our thinking here to everyone in this room, and to everyone in each of our lives, everyone at work, at home, everyone in our neighborhood, our town, our country, and maybe beyond that if you'd like to include everyone on the planet.

"May we all be safe, May we all be happy, May we all be free, May we live in peace." To end this meditation, just take a deep breath in and let it go. Thank you all for being here to share some memories and say farewell to Pat. It means a lot to us. Thank you.

After the service was over, we filed into a nearby restaurant, and it felt nice to gather. My nephews were in college, studying physical therapy, and Ada was thirteen, enamored by them—their strength and smarts, combined. They adored her and everyone settled in chatting as the drinks came. My sister-in-law, Emma, casually shared that they were going to my dad's house for Father's Day, which was just a few days away. "My parents are also coming too," she added. Dan and I exchanged knowing glances but said nothing. Later, I wondered how Emma might feel if I told her that I was going to her dad's house on Father's Day when she herself was not invited?

I'd felt a shift for the last couple of years, really, quite notably during the pandemic when we got vaccinated, encouraged testing, and they did too, but begrudgingly so. They leaned right—hard right. To them, to Jay and Karen, I was a "Lefty-liberal," never to be reached. The relationship between my dad and I (the one I'd dredged up back in college, or perhaps simply created) had withered to nothing. I began to see that I'd been hoping for a father-daughter relationship to develop someday, but it never had, no matter what I did. Now that my mom was gone, I saw more clearly that I'd never truly had a dad. He was my biological father, yes, but he'd decided a long time ago that he would commit to being a part of Karen's family and not mine. From now on, I'm referring to my dad as Jay. Jay and Karen, which is who they are, not dad and mom, never were they dad or mom. I wished them well, sent them love, health, happiness, and peace, and I let them go. I no longer have parents on this earth. I talk to my mom when I look at the sky or see a photo of her face. For many weeks I felt heartache over this new clarity and accepted that pain as

part of this experience we call life. I just put my arms around the pain and love myself more for feeling it. Then, when I floated through the sky in a hot-air balloon, somehow, the joy I felt on that ride burned up all the sadness I'd been holding onto.

Patricia Buchholz, 1944-2023

The Great Wellsville Balloon Rally

"I fly because it releases my mind from the tyranny of petty things." — Antoine de Saint-Exupéry

"Let's get one thing straight. There's a big difference between a pilot and an aviator. One is a technician; the other is an artist in love with flight."— Captain Elrey B. Jeppesen

D an asked me what I wanted for my fiftieth birthday, and I said, "psilocybin." I wanted to have an entirely new experience, a new adventure, if you will. He said he'd talk to his tattoo-artist friend who'd given us mushrooms before. We'd let them shrivel and dry to dust in a drawer, too anxious and responsible to take a whole day out of reality to eat them together. When we saw a hot air balloon soar across the valley early one morning, I suggested a ride in one as an alternative gift. I watched the checkered balloon hover, then rise slowly as I remembered that first magical morning at the Pinkhouse. "That might be easier to procure," he chuckled and got on the phone to find out who to talk to. In a few days he'd contacted a local pilot who'd be flying during the Great Wellsville Balloon rally that was coming up in a few days. GWBR turned sleepy little Wellsville into a wild west carnival crawling with cars, bikes, pedestrians, campers, RVs and more. Main street was closed off for the day to allow artisans and church groups space to sell their goods. If the weather is just right, balloons go up in the early morning, usually around 6:30-7 a.m., as the sun is rising, and the fog is lifting. This Saturday, the fog didn't lift and the wind picked up. Clouds grew like cotton candy in the sky, so a few balloons filled and gave some tethered rides or laid flat, partially filled to allow people to walk into them and look around. By evening, however, the fog and haze had cleared, the winds calmed, and the pilots met on one of the baseball fields surrounded by corn-dog and ice cream trucks, homemade hot-air balloon art and inflatable souvenirs. I was instructed to look for a white truck and a trailer that said Blu-By-U on the side. When I reached Field 3, it was quieter with far fewer people. When my pilot Vicki arrived, she said, "I'm not going to make any promises, but it's looking good." Before I knew it, colorful balloons were being inflated by giant fans while propane torches heated the voluminous bulbs until they stood upright, and crews worked to steady them with ropes. One after another, balloons lifted into the sky. I could feel it: my turn was coming.

It wasn't just my turn to have a fun, unique experience to mark my fiftieth year of life, it was my time to leave all the grave, heavy heartache behind. It was a time to turn everything upside down, a time to feel some levity for once. It was time to feel joy again, to get as close to that other dimension where my mom and her sister were somewhere sipping on lemonade, laughing. If I could just skim against those monumental clouds, she might hear me, like a whisper through a wall. "It's time," one of Vicki's ground crew called out as she motioned to me. I kissed Dan and hurried over to step into the open foothold in the basket, threw my leg over and slid into the tiny, wicker vessel. There was just enough room for the two of us, the giant tank of propane, and a few dangling straps. "Don't touch the red ones," I reminded myself. "You're light tonight, so you're going up quick," Vicki's husband and Chief Ground Crew Officer shouted above the fire-breathing torch suspended just over our heads. "Okay," she chirped, "we're ready!" and up we went, like a buoy in a lake.

As my loved ones shrank below, and the baseball fields and food trucks became model sets of a quaint small town, I realized Vicki was giving me instructions. An overwhelming sense of awe captured my senses. I was awestruck and barely heard her landing procedures until I shook my head to snap out of it long enough to look down at the rope handles and footholds she was referring to in case we had a rough landing. Then, I dove right back in. A child-like sense of curiosity took over, examining every part of the balloon, the basket, the sky, all the other balloons out ahead and below us, the colors, the warmth of the sun, the sensation of floating as if in a row-boat on a still pond. The landscape below had transformed into painterly patterns of color, texture and shape, the setting sun coated everything in gold. "Do you see this, mom?" I whispered, "Can you believe it?" Tears slid down my warm face as I waved to this new world below. You don't see any trash or broken-down rusty cars, litter or cigarette butts, you just see the beauty and balance of this glorious eco-tapestry of our living earth. Like floating along in a boat, you don't feel the wind, because it's moving you with it, steering your ride. The only control you have in a hot air balloon is up and down. We soared above all the other balloons, which seemed smart since you cannot see what's above you in a hot-air balloon, because there's a giant hot-air balloon directly above you, carrying you and your woven vessel. So many other balloons were flying low, as if skimming the treetops. "That's called contour flying," Vicki said, as she pointed out the people and pilots she knew in some of the other balloons around us. The radio clipped to her T-shirt crackled as her husband asked how we were doing and how the traffic looked from up there. "We're doing great," she called out triumphantly, "but the traffic, not so great. I can see you! We're headed over a ridge so you might want to take a right up ahead..." She guided her crew to meet us in an unknown destination. We soared higher, at about three-thousand feet above sea-level, able to soak up the sun-drenched landscape below. "It's like we've got our own vector over here...it's moving us west..." Vicki reported over the radio. All the other balloons pulled to the east and lowered gently to the ground as we continued to rise into the clouds.

"Can you see this, mom, can you see me, do you see this?" My heart kept calling out to the space beyond the clouds. As we passed a forested ridge, we began to descend. I've never experienced a boat ride where you glide over treetops until this. The lighter green, new growth reaching up toward you, atop conifers and maples four stories tall. Everything seemed upside down somehow, unlike life as I knew it. I was filled with joy as much as our blue, green, and pink balloon was filled with hot air. We floated over the trees and slowly sank over a pasture of three horses. "Can you land there?" our crew asked. "No, it's fenced in and there are horses," my aviator replied. I've never looked at running horses from above, like I could jump onto one of their backs like Annie Oakley or Calamity Jane. The pure white horse began to run faster as we approached, and the painted horse ran to keep close to it. The dark horse caught up with them and they began to run in circles, spooked by the fire-breathing noise descending upon them. "We've gotta go back up, they're spooked and stampeding down there," she said. The wind speed was nil down low. We seemed to hover over these three, terrified horses. Soon, we were climbing again and cleared the pasture, traveling toward Pennsylvania. We'd been flying for over half an hour and were now checking gauges, looking for landing sites and communicating more frequently with the crew below.

Vicki's landing procedures delivered upon take-off came back to me as I held onto one of the poles that rose up from the basket, hoping for a safe landing. We spotted an open scrub field with a flat space just beyond some tall willows and decided to make that our landing pad. The Blu-By-U ground crew was parked and ready with a father and son team waiting in the field, arms extended in V's ready to catch us. Joy vibrated up from my toes to the hair on my head with the sight of their open arms. We passed between the willows and touched down with the gentlest landing I never imagined was possible. "We're gonna bounce," Vicki shouted, as I grabbed a rope handle. It was the slowest, softest, moon-landing bounce I'd ever experienced, like an anti-gravity bounce house romp up and down, right into the gloved hands of our crew. We were even buoyant upon landing. I secretly suspected the joy I felt had something to do with it. Vicki gave her balloon enough propane-fueled fire for the crew to walk along us as our basket hovered over the field toward the white truck with the trailer that said Blu-By-U. Smiling faces surrounded us. Our joy had rippled out of us, spilled out of the basket, and flooded the field.

An Amish family sat on a flat-bed wagon behind their horses to watch our landing and a family walked into the field to take pictures. Two Mennonite sisters wearing flower print dresses strode toward us with broad smiles offering to help "clean up" the balloon. This ride was more than my opportunity to celebrate turning fifty, it had been my time to leave the weight of all my grief and pain behind; to feel the levity of joy, to remember how it feels to be genuinely curious about the world, to be filled with wonder about the experience of being alive and part of the harmony of the living, breathing world.

The Ashram

"Desire nothing. Give up all desires and be happy."
— Swami Sivananda

Summer was winding down quickly, and I had the opportunity to meet my dear friend Sand's step brother who is a swami at Sivananda Yoga Ashram in Grass Valley, California. Sand, Cassandra, is one of my best, closest friends: a sister from another mister. When her step mom reached out to me, urging me to meet her son while he was in the Catskills of New York this summer, I couldn't refuse. I decided to register for his class on self-healing at the Sivananda Yoga Ranch in Woodbourne before he returned to California. As the day to leave approached, I felt increasingly nervous about going. Ada had just recovered from Covid-19 again, and although Dan and I were both negative for the virus, there was a knot in my gut that made me doubt. Ada was scheduled to start volleyball and Dan had medical tests that would tell us what was trapped in his lungs. It just wasn't a good time to leave home, but I did anyway.

Dan and Ada lovingly encouraged me to go, to have a good time, because they understood how much it meant to me. When I arrived at the ashram, I was prepared to feel out of place. Everyone was wearing white pants, for starters, and

I was wearing black pants and a bright green T-shirt. I told myself that this was to be expected. I didn't live or work at the ashram, so it was to be expected that I would look and feel like an outsider. I wandered around the beautiful grounds admiring the balance between thoughtful, perennial plantings and wild, native plants and grasses tucked into the hillsides and along stone steps. I made my way to a pond that looked like a clear, black mirror, surrounded with a collar of emerald green. Perfect, I thought, I'm dressed just like this pond. A woman in a bikini emerged from a sauna and stepped onto the floating, wooden dock I was sitting on and slid into the black water. "You're so brave," I remarked. I walked slowly back up the stone steps past a young snake and a beautiful frog, thanking them for sharing their beautiful home and found a lovely dome structure covered in willows. I sat beneath the willows that dutifully wound up the steel dome, creating a shady space that felt safe and welcoming. Sunlight danced through the moving leaves as gentle breezes played the small wind chime that hung from the center of the dome.

I thought of my dear friend Ray. Ray died far too young, and I still miss him every day. The last time I was here, Chad and I were visiting him as he was completing his Yoga Teacher Training. I looked up and said, "Ray, do you remember me? Do you remember this place? Do you remember being here with me before? If you do, please give me a sign that tells me you know that I'm here, that I'm remembering you here in this beautiful place, and that you're with me." Within a minute, a honey-colored dog I'd never seen before loped up the hill, sniffing all around the enclosure, came into the space and sat down right next to my left foot. He didn't just sit down right next to me, this sweet dog leaned into my leg, like an old friend giving me a hug. Like he knew me. Thank you, Ray, I thought, as I stroked the dog. This place is magical if you're awake, aware, appreciating it and communicating with it. But then again, doesn't every place become special when we are aware and appreciative? I felt a bit better about being there, dressed like the pond and with my friend Ray. I went to a yoga class and felt amazing afterward, ate a delicious vegan meal outside and then went to Satsang to meditate and chant with the others.

Raymond Loh was one of the most extraordinary people I've ever known. First generation Chinese-American, he grew up in New York City with his two sisters and extended family. Ray was funny, loved playing all kinds of games, socializing, cracking jokes and connecting with people. He smiled with his whole face, with his whole being. When I first met Ray I was emotionally distraught and felt lost so I came to a Matt Talbot meeting in the basement of a Catholic church in Almond. This was a recovery-style, faith-based meeting that utilized the twelve steps of Recovery but seemed to mix in more assignments and accountability. I was out of my league. Plus, I was suffering from a nasty head cold at the time. Ray greeted me in his friendly way, and at the next meeting he brought me a paper bag filled with herbal tea and traditional Chinese remedies. Ray was compassionate and kind. If anyone in AA needed anything, a sponsor, a ride somewhere, or just a friend to listen, Ray was there. Ray was a recovering addict who had mastered all the recovery steps, knew all the programs and had turned his entire life into one of service to others. In no time at all, Ray and I became close friends. The wind chime played in the wind again as I stroked this lovely dog sent by Ray, and I took a deep breath, missing him but knowing that I was right where I needed to be.

The swami who led Satsang talked about the class she and the other swami (Sand's brother) would be teaching that week. She talked all about the different arms of yoga and how they all help us to heal, not only our physical selves, but the wrong perception we have of ourselves. Finally, she said that Sivananda himself made it very simple, he said, "Do the correct thing, or do what is right, and then go happily." This stayed with me as I went to my room to sleep that night. I started to feel like I had a small collection of nails in my throat and texted Dan and Ada to see how they were feeling. All was well with them, but I didn't sleep all night; my sore throat became more painful, mucus building in my sinuses and filling my throat. I could barely breathe, let alone sleep. As these symptoms worsened, my mind raced faster, repeating what I'd heard at Satsang, replaying one song over and over, "Trouble me," by the 10,000 Maniacs where she's basically asking for trouble because she's strong and she can handle it. I'd focus on a mantra for a while, hoping to calm my mind and fall asleep, but nothing worked. "Trouble me... speak to me...don't mislead me...The calm I feel means a storm is swelling...speak to me...there's no telling where it starts or how it ends..." The song in my head played on as I tossed and turned, becoming more deeply ill and achy as the hours went on. I felt feverish but had no way of taking my temperature or testing for Covid-19, although I knew that was likely since Ada had just recovered from it. I'd tested negative for the virus two days ago, but that could have changed overnight. Please, please, please, I pleaded with the Universe, tell me what to do.

I looked at the clock on my phone. It was 3:52 am and I hadn't slept at all yet. I decided on just making the body comfortable, and I found a way to feel relaxed and melted into a dream state. In the dream, I was in a different country, standing in a small space in an alley with buildings that piled up around me. Ray appeared and we embraced for a long time as he said, "It's about time!" Then I looked up and saw a wall of water, a tidal wave coming straight toward us. I looked up to the right and saw Ada, my beautiful daughter, standing on a balcony above. I could tell that she saw the wave coming too and looked terrified. "Ada," I yelled, as I threw a wooden plank up to her, thinking it was something that would float. As it soared through the air it transformed into a life raft. Then everything went black. The wave hit us.

The morning bell was ringing at the ashram and I woke to realize I'd been asleep for the last hour and a half. The tidal wave, it was clear, was there to tell me that sometimes things that happen are much, much bigger than you, and you simply have no control over the situation. All you can do is do what you think is right in the moment, reach out to others with love and then let go. Okay, I thought, all I can do here and now is test for Covid-19 and then do the right thing after that. I called the reception desk to find out if they had any test kits available. I called, and called, and called. Answering service every time. Finally, I got a person who didn't know but would let me know. Holding the phone in my hand, waiting in my car, watching the time, was simply torture. I was now in the waking, conscious state of a fitful dream, tossing and turning, sweating, and aching like I was last night. Waiting and sitting with the unknown was incredibly tough. After a couple more calls to Venu at the front desk, I burst into tears, admitting that I didn't know what to do, but if I could just test then I would know. He said the swami went out and got some tests, but he didn't know where they were. The swami was very busy, and he'd get back to me when he had one. Waiting and not knowing what to do felt like torture, so I decided to stop torturing myself. Sitting in the way back of my car with the hatch open, I created a little shelter with blankets so I could look at the beautiful trees behind the parking lot. The more I looked with curiosity, the more beauty I saw, and I decided to dialogue with nature.

This is a practice I'm coming to trust and love very much. Looking for something in nature that attracts you—a color, a specially-shaped rock, a lovely tree—anything that grabs your attention, go to it, and sit with it. Be with it in the present moment and notice everything you feel. I was drawn to a horse chestnut tree whose fruits were bright, yellow-green, and spiky—they were simply magnificent. I sat beneath the tree and felt the sunshine on my face. I soon realized that this was helping. I was beginning to feel better. Maybe all of this was just in my head! I noticed a sign that said Durga Temple with an arrow pointing into the woods. I walked to it and saw large, stone steps descending into the forest below. I took one step at a time, noticing how beautiful the wilderness was all around: the bright green ferns, the tree people of all shapes and sizes, the peridot green mosses, the gentle breeze pushing through everything. I continued, one step at a time, until I reached the temple, which was built out onto a rectangular pond. Another black mirror, I noted. I leaned over the wood railing and looked in to see my own reflection looking up. "Do the right thing," it said, "and go happily." I can do that, I thought, and opened the tall, narrow doors of the shrine. Inside were gleaming white floors and statues of deities dressed in red, magenta, and gold, flower petals and candles at their feet. I knelt in a corner and laid my forehead on the cold floor tile. As soon as I felt the cooling touch of the temple floor, a tidal wave of pain and grief rushed out of me, and I wept. After a few minutes, it felt as though I'd flooded the temple with my tears. All the expectations I'd created about this week away—I was going to heal from all my pain, from the grief of losing my mom, from the awareness that I never had a dad, from the fear I felt about Dan's health, the abuse from childhood; I was going to heal everything from this life and then I'd heal all my past lives. I'd make new friends, have new yoga connections, learn new things to teach my students, become friends with swamis, I'd become wise and learned, and I'd return home more confident as a teacher, healed and ready to help everyone else heal their wounds.

It was like I'd created this giant layer cake of expectations, or desires, with colorful frosting between the layers, with tasty ornamental flowers and flourishes at the top. I'd even brought my HAPI drum, imagining I'd bond with people around a campfire. I brought art supplies to create a masterpiece that I could say, while I pointed, "I made that at the ashram." This ridiculously elaborate layer cake of expectations, smashed to the ground, now filled with dirt and gravel, attracting flies and slugs. Somehow, I understood this ruined cake of my own making when my forehead kissed the temple floor. Thank you, I repeated many times as I backed out of the temple. I left a round, clay mandala tile I'd made last year in the grass below the sign for the temple as an offering. It was orange, I reasoned, like the swami's uniforms, so it seemed fitting, and if they didn't like it, they could toss it into the black mirror.

I continued along the footpath, following signs with an Om painted on yellow diamond-shaped trail markers. Each step I noticed something magnificent and alive and felt a part of it all—a Oneness, if you will. At the same time, I felt completely lost, not knowing where I was going, how long the trail would be, or where it would lead, but simply trusted, one step at a time, that I was being led. After a while, the trail markers went right, the footpath leading deeper into the forest. Something in me wanted to go left when I reached a fork in the trail. To the right, there were bright yellow trail markers, to the left, a hill lined with blackberry bushes, but no markers. I felt strongly that if I went left, I'd find the pond I visited yesterday, and then I'd know right where I was. I climbed uphill to the left, picking ripe blackberries, breaking my fast along the way. "Thank you," I continued to say. Soon I noticed tall cattails and knew my instincts were right—this must be the pond, I thought. I stopped to look out at the black water as a Great Blue Heron spread its giant wings only a few feet away from me, pushed off the wooden dock I was sitting on yesterday and lifted into the air. The bird's launch made giant ripples spread across the water and I watched it fly into the treetops. "Thank you," I repeated, knowing that beloved Oneness, as I'm now calling the Universe, or God, has been with me through this all along. This was always the plan. I would take a test soon, see my fears realized in those two, thin, red lines, and drive back home, a failure.

I sobbed on and off, blowing my nose, slowly recovering my senses and sipping water while I drove. I had a four hour drive ahead of me. One of my brilliant stepson's songs from Spotify came on in the music shuffle. *Upset*, the screen read. "Yes, I am, sweet Ry. I am upset, and you've felt it too," I thought aloud. I'm going to give myself permission to be upset today. After another hour of upset, I needed a change. Listening to the Happiness podcast with Dr. Robert Puff is still something Dan and I share together, so I thought that might help this hot mess I'd become overnight. Dr. Puff reminded me of something I already know; that we cannot control what happens to us in life, but we can control how we respond to it. The kind of person you are is always more important than whatever it is you're doing. So, I drive on, ready to learn the lessons of this experience, ready to grow and heal in whole new ways. These challenges I'm experiencing are not here because some distant deity placed them there. They're here because I asked them to be here. How do I heal? This has been an essential question for me for as long as I can remember. The physical manifestation of an illness is the way for me to experience one aspect of healing, to truly appreciate the process by living through it. Covid-19, like any illness, allows for that possibility.

I'm doing it. I'm healing, one day at a time, just by resting, noticing, and responding to my needs. I'm fortunate to not have to work right now, that I have the luxury of staying home in a peaceful environment. This helps tremendously, and for that I'm very thankful. How can I heal totally and completely, from this life and all the others I've been through? How do I then help others to heal and live a life of wholeness and love? By doing nothing more than trusting in the process I'm going through and listening to what it is I need, I *am* healing. If I'm winded from walking, I stop. I breathe deeply and rest. If I'm hungry, I eat. I know I feel better when I eat something healthy, so I do my best, but there's no need for any judgment, I just eat until I feel like I've had enough. I pause to feel grateful and say so, either internally, or out loud to the sky, to the day, to whoever's listening.

Today is day five healing from this most recent Covid-19 visitation. I feel myself healing more every day and begin to realize that I needed to be here to heal. I needed to be home on Heron Hill, watching the changing sky, the birds, resting and appreciating all that surrounds me here. Free from any distractions, demands or expectations that would be present in a class at the ashram, I can be fully relaxed, at ease and present to witness this process of healing at its own pace.

There was a part of me that was racing ahead. The part of me that was so tired of feeling trapped by my mom's illnesses and heartache. The friend in me who longed for Ray, for a true friend. The child in me who needed my dad's stories and stability but was never invited to partake in them. The part of me who wanted to be totally and finally healed from all the movement of this life, all the heartache. So naturally, reaching for some other place like the ashram made sense to me. Reaching for some other teacher, besides myself, some other class or retreat to dive into, was that part of me that was afraid to trust again. I trust that being here now, at home with myself, and by myself, is where all my healing will occur. My Heron tattoo is pointing right at it. It is from within the blackest depths of my own heart, like the mysterious depths of the pond, where my healing originates and is also received. I've been led here, to Heron Hill, to my home, to heal.

In the morning I will awaken fully to my Self.

I will be healed completely, body, mind, and spirit.

I will know who I am, because I am free, I am connected, I am home, and finally, I am truly, undeniably, happy.

The Timeless Now

"Many people are so imprisoned in their minds that the beauty of nature does not really exist for them. They might say, "what a pretty flower," but that's just a mechanical labeling. Because they are not still, not present, they don't truly see the flower, don't feel its essence, its holiness—just as they don't see themselves, don't feel their own essence, their own holiness." — Eckhart Tolle

And then, life keeps happening, and you realize you're not healed completely but that healing is this continual process of becoming, of adapting, changing and transforming who you are. This continual process of letting go. As long as love is at the center, as long as you can tap into the here and now, with wonder and curiosity, with awe for the great mystery of this life, then... you're home. Yoga and meditation practice reminds me to keep coming home to my heart, to my own, true self.

Today I am so very thankful
for my health, for my beautiful daughter and
her strength, her resiliency, and
for Dan and how kind and tender he is to us.
I'm thankful for Riley, driving alone in the dark
returning from college to be with family,
to spend some time with us.

I'm grateful for the pink in the clouds at sunset that
mirrored the pink of this morning's sunrise, and
for those few, quiet moments
I sat in wonder,
appreciating it all.

A friend of mine is an energy healer. During a healing session, she cut the energetic chords that connected me to my mom, my dad, and all others-everyone. When the session was over, she assured me, I would "stand up with my energy alone." She repeated this several times as she walked around me in circles. She told me as soon as I thought of someone, that chord would grow back, but only if I wanted it to. After her magic was done, I felt different. Lighter, like somehow I'd taken off a weighted suit and could walk with a little bounce, with ease. I didn't feel the lifelong sorrow in my chest for my mother's perpetual illness and disease. I felt free! I thought of Dan, Ada, Riley, and Thor and knew that those chords were healthy ones, full of life and flexibility, of alignment and love. I'm dancing and taking days off, manifesting, and resting. I'm so blessed and strong, healthy and happy–meanwhile the world is at war, and there is unspeakable suffering. It would be easy to get lost in that darkness again. Trying to change others, trying to change the world. Sharing yoga and mindfulness helps ground me and remind me that I'm doing what I can. Nurturing that peace inside me, sharing it with others, encouraging loving-kindness, listening more closely, that is what I'm doing now. Breathing in the world just as it is, breathing out peace, love and acceptance. Feeling a true freedom, happiness, and gratitude for everyone and everything that helped me arrive here, beneath the Herons' path in the sky.

If I could manifest anything I wanted, I would bring my daughter a certainty that she is loved, cherished, and needed in this world, that she has a home inside her own heart that is ever present and infinitely expanding. I would bring my stepson Riley his own recording studio and creative space that has all the creative people and tools to help him realize his creative dreams. I would bring peace to every village and town, every county and state, and every nation so every human would see themselves when they looked at each other. I would bring us all to that dream of pure bliss, feeling connected to oneness and infinitely larger than this small physical realm. I would manifest new forests protected for millennia, new species who ate plastic and gave children rides. I would create an adventure with my beautiful daughter where we bond and make wonderful memories together, explore and learn together. I would manifest a trip to India to learn more about yoga and meditation and somehow be of service. I would make new friends who collaborate with me creatively, where we help lift each other to new heights of expression and growth. I would invite a refugee family to live with us until they were ready and able to move into their own home but remain close friends forever, as they find more families who stay with us during their time of need, creating a trusted safe haven here in Wellsville. I would be a healer who connects people to one another and to their greatest source of healing within. I would be a massage therapist, an artist, a writer, speaker, singer, gardener, herbalist, environmentalist and maker of magic. In order to do all this, I know I need to let go of my fear of death. I don't want to be so afraid of dying that I never truly live. I still have to make some important connections. There is still more healing work for me to do. I need to reconcile the two moms that influenced my life like opposing magnetic forces for the past fifty years.

Karen Wallace had very long, brown hair when she married my dad. It was twisted and wrapped up in a bun on their wedding day. My mom had short, cropped hair. She was a smart, independent business woman, my mom. Soon after Jay and Karen were married, Karen cut all her hair off. Her hair cut reminded me of my mom's. She *looked* like my mom. When I was a kid, I would imagine that something my mom did or said, something my mom wanted, would come through Karen like a force. Karen would buy something because my mom wanted her to. Karen would declare that she liked a song playing on the radio, not because she did, but because *my mom did*. If my mom saw something and said, "Oh, your father would like that," then Karen would buy it a few days later and when I saw it, I'd know that it was actually from my mom.

One year, my mom took my brother and I Christmas shopping for my dad. We didn't have our own money yet, so she wanted to help us in giving him something when we visited for the holidays. We got him a brown organizational caddy for his car. I thought it was brilliant! Practical and thoughtful, he was sure to love it! I felt so proud presenting him with our gift, but Karen was not having it. She knew my mom had bought it and would think of her every time they were in the car. "No," she said, "We can't accept this," and she made us take it back to my mom with a message to never buy him anything again. After that I began to pretend that what my mom wanted for us kids or my dad would somehow magically come through Karen's consciousness, and without knowing it, she would be doing just what my mom wanted.

Karen loved to shop. She loves Jo-Ann fabrics and yard sales and thrift shops and church basements and SPCA fundraisers. She often brings bags of clothing to us to "Look through and take what we want," as if they're gifts but it's more like evidence of her shopping addiction. Rather than refuse and listen to her insist on "just looking through it," we sort through the clothes and keep an item or two, pass on the rest and move on with our lives. I'm less and less likely to keep any item found in one of Karen's bags nowadays, since I don't need or want any of it. But recently, I did. I kept one gray, wool sweater with a large Black swan on the front. There was just something about it. I wasn't sure why I needed to keep this sweater from Karen's bag until I came across the story of Buddha and the swan.

Apparently, thousands of years ago, Buddha was walking through the forest as a young boy. His cousin was out hunting nearby and shot a beautiful swan with his bow and arrow. Buddha found the wounded swan before his cousin did and didn't know who'd injured the bird. Filled with sorrow and compassion for the beautiful bird, Buddha held it gently and carefully removed the arrow. He then bandaged the bloody wing and held it for a long time, helping the swan heal and recover from the trauma. Eventually, the cousin appeared and shouted to Buddha, "That's my swan, give it to me! I shot it, so it's mine!" Buddha refused to hand over the frightened bird and the two argued for quite some time. Unable to reach an agreement, the young boys took their argument to the royal court. Buddha's father was a wealthy king and had a wise elder he consulted in cases like these. The old man listened carefully to both sides of the story and decided that because Buddha had helped save the life of the swan, that it should belong to him. Buddha's cousin had acted against the swan's life, attempting to kill it, and therefore did not deserve the right to own the swan. I don't see myself as the Buddha in this story, or the cousin, or even the white swan, which seems to represent innocence. I'm not the white swan, but maybe I was once, as a child.

When a child feels unwanted by her own family, that is very painful, and it can feel like your heart is black inside, like a great void. Just as Morrissey said, "I wear black on the outside because I feel black on the inside." For decades of my life, I felt the pain of this kind of disconnection and loss. This emotional pain was also physical. I felt it intensely in both my heart and in my throat. I felt searing pain in my gut, cracking teeth and hair loss as I endured a marriage I couldn't allow myself to leave. As Brene Brown writes in Atlas of the Heart, "...feelings of disconnection actually share the same neural pathways with feelings of pain. Current neuroscience research shows that the pain and feelings of disconnection are often as real as physical pain, and just as healing physical pain requires describing it, talking about it and sometimes getting professional help, we need to do the same thing with emotional pain." I pull on the sweater with the black swan on the front and remember a visit I had with my mom in the nursing home many months before.

Pre-Parkinson's, my mom would have been aghast at the giant heron tattoo permanently etched into my arm, but full-blown Parkinson's mom just noticed it with a child-like curiosity. "Oh," she said, on that blazing hot day in Elderwood's courtyard, looking at my exposed arms. "You're a black swan." I corrected her and talked dreamily about Great Blue Herons and how they flew directly over our new house. But somehow, after she left this world, she sent me this sweater through Karen's hands just to let me know that even though I'd lost my innocence and youth in the blink of an eye, I'd always belonged to her. And because I belonged to my mother, and was truly loved by her, in spite of all her mistakes, I can now belong to myself.

Sources

Beattie, M.,1986, Codependent No More: How to Stop Controlling Others and Start Caring for Yourself, Hazelden Foundation.

Brown, B., 2021, Atlas of the Heart: Mapping Meaningful Connection and the Language of Human Experience, Random House.

Karbo, K., 2018, In Praise of Difficult Women: Life Lessons from 29 Heroines Who Dared to Break the Rules, National Geographic.

Paquette, W., & Woelfel, J. & Woelfel, M., 2018, The Pink House: The Legendary Residence of Edwin Bradford Hall and His Succeeding Generations in Wellsville, New York, New Dominion Press.

Skoglund, S. (1980) Radioactive Cats, St. Louis Art Museum, St. Louis, Missouri, U.S.A.

About The Author

Kristin Wall Buchholz is a New York State certified Art Teacher who has taught all ages, from young children to adults, using hands-on, experiential teaching methods. She is a graduate of Syracuse University and the Harvard Graduate School of Education. Kristin is also a certified Yoga Teacher who combines different disciplines of yoga and meditation for the purpose of healing. An artist, naturalist, and gardener, she is establishing a small homestead and finally putting down roots. She lives in Wellsville, NY, with her family. Kristin's newly established Yoga studio, known as Heron Hill Yoga, overlooks the foothills of the Allegheny mountains. "Guided Migrations" is her first book.